MEDITATION &
RELAXATION

MEDITATION & RELAXATION

AUTHOR: *Mariëlle Renssen*
CONSULTANT: *Natalia Baker*

NEW HOLLAND

First published in 2003 by
New Holland Publishers
London • Cape Town • Sydney • Auckland
www.newhollandpublishers.com

86 Edgware Road
London W2 2EA
United Kingdom

80 McKenzie Street
Cape Town 8001
South Africa

14 Aquatic Drive
Frenchs Forest, NSW 2086
Australia

218 Lake Road
Northcote, Auckland
New Zealand

ISBN 1 84330 003 6 (HB)
ISBN 1 85974 998 4 (PB)

Managing Editors: Claudia Dos Santos, Simon Pooley
Managing Art Editor: Richard MacArthur
Designer: Sheryl Buckley
Illustrator: Jessica Breytenbach

Consultant: Natalia Baker

Reproduction by Hirt & Carter (Cape) Pty Ltd
Printed and bound in Singapore by Craft Print International Ltd

2 4 6 8 10 9 7 5 3 1

DISCLAIMER

THIS BOOK IS DEDICATED TO

all those on our planet who show the way of love, peace and wisdom through their commitment to the practice of meditation

C O N T E N T S

INTRODUCTION

THE wisdom of the various meditative traditions available to us today goes back many thousands of years. It has been passed down through the centuries by Yogis, sages and saints of both the East and the West – all ordinary human beings, who, through their own difficult lives, set out to search for an inner truth by meditating rigorously and with great determination in their earnest quest for a happier, more fulfilled life. Their writings provide the most prolific and authoritative source of meditative knowledge in the world today.

The most well-recognized of these early philosophers is the Buddha, Gautama Siddhartha, who is credited with first establishing the Buddhist tradition. Although this tradition has been integrated into Eastern philosophies for centuries, recently there has been a surge of rekindled interest in the Western world.

The need today among an increasing number of people to find ways to cope with the increased pace of their lives is forcing them to look toward a more contemplative form of relaxation. Most of us live in a society based on Western ideals: advancing our knowledge through science and technology to produce tangible, fact-based results; working in businesses that strive to serve capitalist-driven economies; and being caught up in a faster pace as a direct result of our technological progress. This brings about a need to slow down, still ourselves, and focus inward.

Meditation is the most extraordinarily powerful means of changing one's life for the better. It teaches us to still the mind's uncontrolled thoughts and tame our fluctuating emotions, making room for a clarity that allows the instinctive wisdom and intuition that is within all of us to arise. An uncluttered mind promotes clearer thinking, better problem-solving and more focused decision-making.

MOST people are like a falling leaf that drifts and turns in the air, flutters, and falls to the ground. But a few others are like stars which travel one defined path: no wind reaches them, they have within themselves their guide and path. Among all the wise men, of whom I knew many, there was one who was perfect in this respect. I can never forget him. He is Gotama, the Illustrious One who preaches this gospel. Thousands of young men hear his teachings every day and follow his instructions every hour, but they are all falling leaves; they have not the wisdom and guide within themselves.

— Herman Hesse's **Siddhartha**

ORIGINS OF MEDITATION

THERE are records of formal practices resembling meditation dating back thousands of years, although in those times meditative practices remained the realm of higher sages. Ancient civilizations were mainly theocratic – governance of the people was according to divine law and led by deities or priesthoods. Among the Egyptians and the Greeks, they were pharaohs, high priests and priestesses while the Native Indians and Chinese had their shamans, diviners, healers, and medicine men.

THE ANCIENT CIVILIZATIONS

Although there are no extensive records of formal meditation practices among the Egyptian civilizations, we do know they placed great importance in their dreams, and the omens they contained. Temples called serapeums existed around 4000 years ago in which people practised 'dream incubation'. A person would sleep in the temple in the hope of receiving a portentous dream which would later be interpreted by the oracles or priests. The significance here is the intense

Left The gigantic proportion of many Buddhist statues is believed to reflect the Buddha's spiritual stature.

A GREAT HISTORICAL TRADITION

rituals that used to precede the incubant's night in the temple: these included fasting, bathing and anointing with oils, and praying — in itself a form of meditation.

Dream incubation, together with its preparatory rituals, was also practised in Greece, although the Greek focus was more on healing and finding medical cures, by calling on the gods of sleep, Hypnos and Morpheus.

THE TRIBAL SPIRIT WORLD

Because tribal societies live so close to Nature and are exposed to the vagaries of weather and powerful natural phenomena such as drought and destructive winds, lightning and thunderstorms, they believe in a world of powerful spirit forces. Their primal form of religion embraces ritual ceremonies of drumming and dancing which produce states of ecstasy and

Above **A painting of Indian god Jina, seated in the lotus posture, the traditional pose for meditation.**

visions through which the spirit world makes itself heard. Important are the shamans, who are specialists of these trance states and through them are able to communicate with the spirits. However, these states cannot strictly be compared with a true meditative state. In early hunter-gatherer societies, tribe members developed keen intuitive abilities, particularly during their hunt rituals which involved many hours — and sometimes days — of intense calm, concentration and heightened awareness as they tracked down their prey. Attaining this mind state is a key aspect of meditation.

MONASTICISM

The monastic traditions of religious contemplation included some of what are known as the 'universal' religions, such as Christianity, where monks and nuns would enter a monastery to lead a reclusive existence of asceticism (fasting and celibacy) during which they would pray for hours. Solitary contemplation was one of their forms of meditation.

HINDU INFLUENCES

Although Buddhism is the path most closely associated with meditation, it actually grew out of the Hindu tradition, which has been in existence as far back as three millennia BCE. Archaeological excavations have unearthed a statue dating back to this period of a Hindu god deep in contemplation in the yogic position.

The idea of combining yoga with meditation reinforces the Hindu belief in humankind as one with the Universe; physical, mental and spiritual, when harmoniously united, become wholly integrated with cosmic energies.

BUDDHA, THE ENLIGHTENED ONE

Buddhism is said to be founded by Prince Gautama Siddhartha, who was born to a Hindu family in 560BCE. (Of the two main sects that developed, Theravada and Mahayana Buddhism, the Theravadins talked of several other Buddhas, but Gautama is undeniably the most well recognized.) It is in the East, therefore, that meditation was initially equated with inner spiritual discovery.

Gautama Siddhartha, despite the affluent, protected life he was living, still experienced a sense of inner dissatis-faction; he was horrified, too, by the illness, old age and death that everyone faced. Deciding to leave behind his life of education and luxury, his family and friends, he set out as a simple mendicant — depending on the charity of others — to explore the deeper yearning of his soul and seek true knowledge with the mystics of his time. To achieve this, he first practised Yoga, thereafter turning to extreme asceticism. However, it was during this time that his health rapidly deteriorated, and it eventually brought him to the realization that extremes were not the answer to self-knowledge.

Siddartha Gautama embarked on the now famous style of meditation, the 'middle path'. This simple but profound approach came to him after a boat sailed by on which a musician was explaining to a student that one should keep the strings of one's sitar 'not too loose and not too tight' in order to produce the best notes.

In Bodh Gaya, Gautama settled under a fig tree to meditate and it was here that he gained self-knowledge and became enlightened. Today the tree is known as the 'bodhi tree', or 'tree of enlightenment'. Having become a Buddha — 'the awakened, or enlightened, one' — he fast gained a following and his teachings spread across most of Asia.

Opposite **The Buddhist path sets out to sublimate the ego, aided by regular meditative practices.**

Right **Objects such as these, arranged with Zen simplicity, are used in meditation to encourage mental clarity.**

ZEN BUDDHISM

Based on the Buddhist tradition, Zen is a school of thought which, although originating in India during the lifetime of Siddhartha Gautama, was brought to Japan from China in the 11th century. (Buddhism was first introduced to China in the first century CE by Bodhidarma, a meditation leader in southern India of a sect combining elements of Taosim with Mahayana Buddhism.)

Over decades, Zen Buddhism gradually infused every aspect of life, from the home, garden and natural environment to the hours spent in contemplation of one's essential nature to gain enlightenment, or satori.

Zen ideals encompass simplicity, tranquillity and calm — all reflected in Japan's serene minimalist interiors and simplified gardens which focus on quality in shape, texture and finish. These values are also seen in the pared-down but exquisite flower arrangements, known as ikebana. This sparse visual approach to life is based on the belief that, by removing all that is not absolutely essential from one's life, the body, mind and spirit experience greater clarity and are open to greater creativity since the immediate environment offers no distractions. The austerity of Zen leads to increased concentration, intuition and insight.

Learning the art of awareness forms the basis of Zen principles, and aids

the individual toward enlightenment. This is achieved more easily by shedding one's attachment to worldly things, and in getting rid of clutter one is able to focus more pointedly on meditation.

An important teaching of Zen is being able to turn a daily mundane task into a type of meditational ritual by becoming intensely aware of every physical moment and infusing the act with a sense of importance. This is no more evident than in the Japanese tea-making ceremony (see p88), *cha ho yu* — The Way of Tea. If individuals perfect this, they can at any point control and clear the mind of unwanted and unsettling thoughts.

THE *purpose of meditation is that we leave the intellect and enter a state of 'beingness' with ourselves.*

— Natalia Baker

MEDITATION *does not come easily. A beautiful tree grows slowly. One must wait for the blossom, the ripening of the fruit and the ultimate taste. The blossom of meditation is an expressible peace that permeates the entire being. Its fruit . . . is indescribable.*

— Swami Vishnu-devananda

LET *the past fall away*
Let the future fall away
Let the present moment be perfect.

— Steven Norval

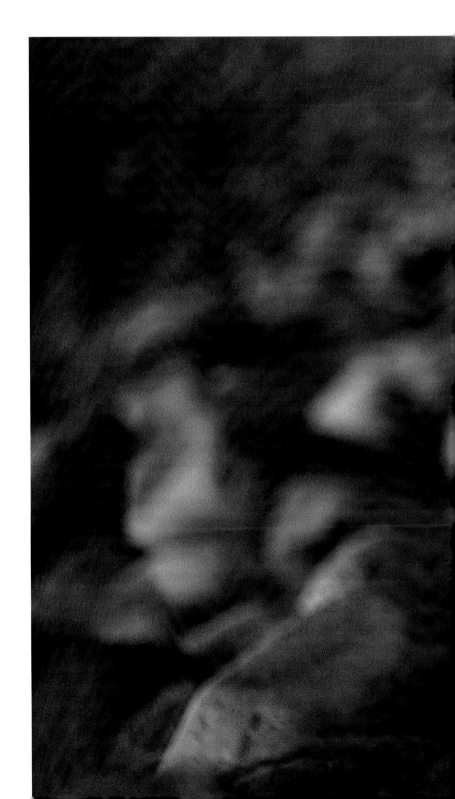

A Means to De-stress

BENEFITS OF MEDITATION

PEOPLE *who start out to meditate for the first time could find that beginning with a simple routine of as little as five minutes a day makes a marked difference in their lives.*

Meditation, in the simplest terms, is about being in a 'state of nothingness'. In the light of the frenetic pace most of us endure in our busy, stress-filled lives, this is an enviable state to be in. In setting out to quieten the flux of thoughts which create a constant chatter within the mind, often stimulated by emotions, meditation succeeds in bringing you to a state of inner calm. You will find that as you relax and centre yourself, your physical and mental health improves.

DE-STRESS YOUR LIFE

It is well documented that meditation brings about many physical benefits to the individual. Deep regulated breathing increases the supply of oxygen through the body and also calms the nervous system; this improved flow of the breath and oxygen-rich blood brings down the heart rate (it doesn't need to pump so hard to supply the body with its needs). It has been proved, too, that a session of deep controlled breathing will lower high blood pressure almost immediately.

Regular meditation helps you to free your head from its constant mental chatter, leading to more focused, uncluttered thinking and more effective decision-making. Being more in control over your mind and any compulsive reactions allows you to have a clearer perspective on situations and also does away with auto-response judgements which are embedded within all of us through social conditioning. Our obsessive thinking processes — and the emotions driven by them — are predominantly driven by our ego, that part of the self which holds all our programming and conditioning. These are the result of our individual life experience which moulds our personal perception of the world and how we fit into it. Any emotional wounding locked in the ego can create masks; it can also motivate our actions, and cause us to confirm rigidly to societal morals and codes.

Meditation is the powerful tool that can still the mental sparring of the egotistical mind, and ultimately lead to an authentic self living a more peaceful and relaxed existence.

Stillness within creates calm without

By giving your mind the time and space to reduce its overactivity, you will find that you are motivated by your own common sense or inner wisdom. Thus, you learn to operate from a personal reality that is more 'true' because you are tapping into purely intuitive faculties. However, intuition does not arise when the mind is cluttered with analysis, criticisms, judgements and programmed perceptions.

Eastern thought sees intuition as 'higher wisdom' because it is not influenced by the mind's rationalizing, analytical processes. Intuition is a higher form of intelligence because it draws on insight, wisdom and understanding. Ultimately, you align your inner world with the outer world, and so live with greater integrity.

Essentially, the meditative state is an alive, calm, focused presence in the moment — an inner stillness and awareness of 'being' on a non-rational level as the cognitive mind

doesn't come into play. It is an interesting fact that people who find true and lasting success in life, not just in business, all have some meditative aspect, or a focused outlet for relaxation, in their lives whether it is Yoga, dancing, swimming, golf, gardening, or fishing.

Opposite and below **Many relaxation activities have a meditational quality about them because they demand a certain focus, a single-pointed concentration on the task, which distracts the mind from its normal mental activity. The way Nature, too, fully engages the senses is good for diverting the mind from the fetters of its daily anxieties.**

LEARN TO STILL THE MIND

MAKING THE FIRST MOVE

Everyone can practise meditation — even children and the elderly are becoming interested today. No particular skills or attributes are required; all you have to do is sit down and 'be'.

The means to start training the mind for this state of 'being' is concentration. This implies doing an activity quietly and slowly, without being distracted, and in which you can focus your attention single-pointedly — that is, thinking of only one thing at a time. The difficulties today are that people's lives are filled with so much activity — even recreational and relaxation pursuits can be competitive and sport- or business-oriented.

Being in a state of 'non-doing' teaches you to cut through the mental chatter, termed 'discursiveness' because it's an endless internal conversation moving between decision and indecision, swinging between moods and emotions, seesawing from hope to fear. Such emotions influence the decisions you make and the actions you take in life.

Right **Any peaceful spot in your home can be turned into a suitable space for some quiet contemplation.**

Tibetans have a saying: 'You can either cover the world in leather or you can just cover your feet in leather.' In other words, narrow the ambit of your vision and sharpen the focus: you need only control your mind in order to properly manage your entire life.

You may start out feeling that your concentration is fairly good, but once you try to meditate you immediately find it is impossible to keep your mind clear of thoughts for more than a few seconds at a time. Trying to focus it on something for any length of time is at first very difficult. Thoughts simply won't stop coming in.

Don't become despondent at this point. You shouldn't approach meditation thinking that you will magically be able to do it first time around. It is like taking up a new sport — it takes a lot of practice before you feel confident in what you are doing. There will be times when you feel that you are making no progress; however each time you practise makes the next session that little bit easier — and undeniably makes a difference to the quality of your meditation. The importance is to acknowledge the need to calm your mind's mental turbulence and make a start at meditating.

FOCUS, CLARITY AND CALM

You can quieten the chatter by not being drawn into any argument your mind is having with itself. Initially, concentration techniques will help you divert your attention from the thoughts as they come up, teaching you to get used to focusing on only one thing at a time. You learn to neither engage in nor reject the turbulent mental activity of your mind, rather to recognize and accept what is there, acknowledge each thought as it arises and gently push it aside. In this way you learn to let go of conflicting emotional responses, thought patterns, or entrenched beliefs when they arise. You need to recognize the paradox that perhaps there is more than one answer, conflicting answers, or even no answer at all.

Much, much later you may have trained your mind to the point where it thinks of nothing at all. If you do achieve this, even with the absence of thought you will be aware of the power of the mind in its stronger, clearer state. You could sometimes experience a rare glimpse of the mind's magic: everything seems suddenly to become quiet, your vision sharpens and brightens, and an incredible sense of peace and well-being pervades you. You experience an overwhelming sense of knowing that leaves you feeling wonderfully revit-

alized and happy. The practice of meditation trains the mind to more easily access and be in this state.

These small windows of clarity make you realize that you have an inborn wisdom that is not gained through learning or experience. It is beyond the control of logic and reason. You are essentially tapping into behaviour and intuition that is latent within you to guide and direct your actions. For most people, however, the layers of habitual patterning and social conditioning, which create mistrust and fear within them, need to be peeled away first. People need to learn to trust themselves more fully.

Thus through meditation you aim to reach a purer reality because the mind in this peaceful state — pure awareness of self without the distraction or influence of thought — relies solely on its own inherent power and wisdom.

POWERFUL INFLUENCE OF INNER SERENITY

The first major achievement is the decision to turn to meditation; it indicates a willingness to be proactive in taking responsibility for yourself. You are prepared to face your inner self and attempt to harmonize your external physical world with your inner mental and spiritual world. Meditation teaches you to be more honest with yourself, so you are more likely to take a more congruent approach to life.

Above **Meditation, as with all skills, becomes easier the more you practise. Among the Buddhist community, this skill is learnt from an early age.**

The two qualities associated with all meditative traditions are compassion and wisdom. They are attained through a true understanding of your mind states. This can come about if you commit yourself to: sitting at first for 20 minutes (this can become longer as you practise) and harness the mind; achieving a calm peace in which decisions arise from within the true inner self and are well thought out; doing away with wasted energy spent on stressful thoughts and mental arguments; seeing things from a new, creative perspective because you are in control of your mind.

Scientifically, it is known that brain wave-patterns work on four levels: beta, alpha, theta and delta. Beta controls the analytical, logical, deductive qualities of the left brain; it is where physical activity and rational thought takes place. The alpha right brain is creative, imaginative, and artistic; it is also where intuition, feeling and innate intelligence stem from. This is the best level for meditation. Endorphins, chemicals that promote feelings of wellbeing in a person and have been proven to boost the immune system, are released in the alpha state. It is a much slower-pulsating brain wave in which you reach a very deep mental stillness, and access true imagination, inspiration and artistic ideas. It is at delta level, the slowest-pulsating brain wave, that experienced Yogis attain a state of 'absolute ecstasy'.

Meditation can also influence and stimulate the body's powerful self-healing mechanisms. It is becoming widely accepted today, even within orthodox medicine circles, that a person is capable of using positive mental attitudes together with the body's own healing powers to initiate a healing process.

As the human being is an energy system (see p56), so thought has its own energy vibrations, with the potential to affect the body's physical, mental and spiritual layers. Eastern concepts of the body consisting of energy channels called meridians, along which are seven main energy centres called chakras, are being accepted more and more by the West. It is believed that any blockages in the meridians or imbalances in the chakras manifest themselves as illnesses in the physical body. Illness is increasingly referred to these days as 'dis-ease' — referring not to any bacterial or viral infection, but rather to the disharmony existing in the meridians or chakras stimulated by the physical body and mental/spiritual bodies being out of alignment. It is a state of the body 'not being at ease' with itself. Through visualization techniques and measured breathing, meditation can restore harmony to these areas.

On an emotional level, meditation strengthens a sense of trust in yourself. The more you meditate and learn to relax, the more you become attuned to your powerful intuition and learn to trust your innate wisdom. It teaches you to be more discerning about the external influences of the media, advertising, people's opinions, and others' expectations of you. By making space in your mind, you give any narrow points of view you may have room to expand; this leads to greater perspective and you eventually can 'let go' of certain judgements or entrenched opinions. Meditation teaches you to move away from the standard 'knee-jerk' reaction, referred to as 'reactivity', which is the result of conditioning and habitual thoughts that have become deeply ingrained. No thought process is required for them to emerge — they are a conditioned reflex.

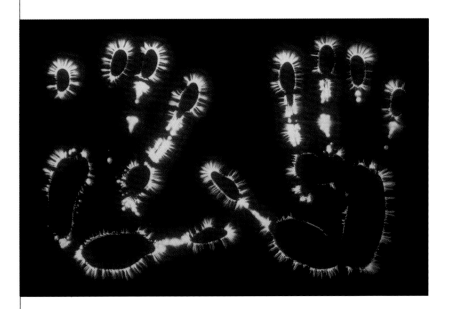

Left Captured on film via the process of Kirlian photography, a pair of hands responds to an applied electric field; light is being emitted as photons from the electrical interaction.

MEDITATIVE RELAXATION

Relaxation is the body's own form of meditation. Movement is slowed, muscles release tension, and aches dissolve. But to gain the most out of your relaxation, a degree of mindfulness is necessary; meditation and relaxation are therefore inextricably linked. You need to be fully present with complete awareness in the moment, using all your senses.

In relaxing your body, you need to relax the mind at the same time — but not through 'tuning out' since you then become detached from the essence of true relaxation. It is important not to become divorced from your senses; you need to be fairly alert and in tune with the process.

We fall into stressful situations with such ease, today — malfunctioning electronic equipment or computer viruses in the workplace when we have a deadline to meet, a tense meeting, conflict with a colleague, being caught in a traffic jam when we're in a hurry to get somewhere — but how

quickly, too, one forgets how simple it is to deal with that stress if one gives oneself the opportunity. Even a few minutes of deep breathing, calming and stilling the body and mind, can do the trick.

You will gain much if you supplement your personal progress in meditation by reading books on the subject, and attending lectures and courses, as you will be introduced to truths that have been tried and tested by others. You can learn from such people by applying the techniques in your own meditation to see if they work for you.

GAINING AWARENESS IN DAILY LIFE

As a preliminary exercise try to notice what activities in the areas of work, sport, hobbies and recreation would be conducive to meditation. Which might be difficult, and which impossible? Try mindfulness and awareness during your different daily activities and see how this could serve to enhance what you are doing or help you to relax at the same time.

Look around at others and see how certain activities demand certain states of mind. When you approach other people throughout your day see how much awareness they have of you and their environment, how much you have and what situations can change this.

Note how few silences there are when people are together and how people will quickly start talking to fill up what they feel to be embarrassing spaces in-between.

Take three deep breaths at any time of day, slowly and deeply exhaling all your tension, anxiety and stress away.

Above **We need to learn that deep, controlled breathing — which calms the nervous system, and our response to stress — can help us cope with the frenetic pace of modern life.**

WHEN *you keep up your daily practice of turning your eye within, you open up a channel in your being that makes you more aware than you were before. In the same way that you train a muscle to obey your will, so too can you train the mental body to obey the will of consciousness.*

— Judy Finch

THE *purpose of meditation is that man leave the intellect and enter a state of his own existence, beingness with himself and thereby with the Higher Self or God Self.*

— Judy Finch

PATIENTLY, *little by little, a man must free himself from all mental distractions with the aid of intelligent will.*

— Bhagavad-Gita

STARTING OUT

WHEN TO MEDITATE

NOWADAYS we generally have to fit things into our lives when we have the time, and obviously it is better to do your meditation whenever you can rather than none at all.

It is a good idea in the beginning to try meditating at various times of the day. In this way, you will find your optimum period — that is, when your mind is at its most relaxed but it is also fairly alert.

EARLY MORNING is a great time to practise since the mind is relaxed and fresh, and the day crisp and beautiful. There are likely to be few distractions and noises at this time. After months, or years, getting up early becomes addictive — and rightly so, as this is the most wonderful, energy-charged time of day.

MIDDAY is also a good time as it's an opportunity to do something positive with your lunch break, which is often wasted because it's such an in-between time or period of limbo. An added advantage is that it helps you to relax, focus and recharge your spirits, enabling you to deal more effectively with your energy which for most people tends to spiral downward in the afternoon.

EVENINGS are an option as this is when the pressures of the day have been dealt with and you may have time to spare. However, be careful of meditating before you go to sleep since for many people it can be very energizing; this could have you lying wide-eyed in the early hours of the morning. On the other hand, if you do awake in the night and cannot sleep, meditating at this time will relax you and you will sleep soundly afterwards.

Few people can successfully meditate in their beds because it is too closely associated with the sleep state. It is more difficult to make a focused inner connection.

Some people find that at this time of evening, they tend to be very tired and will fall asleep during their meditation. If this is the case, a good practice is to meditate with your eyes open, focusing on a point some distance away from you which is slightly lower than eye level.

WEEKENDS are a good time to try an extended period of meditation (initially do this on one day only). Try an extra half of your allotted time — or double your time if you feel you can. Like any new activity, it is helpful to draw up a practice timetable; then make sure you stick to it.

Left **Early mornings are often best for meditating, because it requires a fresh and focused mind.**

Right **If you are struggling to find quiet time to yourself, an hour of bathtime solitude could be the answer.**

Tips

- Meals should be very light (for example, fruit or soup) if you need to eat before a meditation.
- It is best not to meditate on a full stomach as the body's energy is directed to the digestive process and you tend to feel tired.
- Fix a regular time for meditation to outwit the cunning of the mind which will find many plausible excuses and 'more important' things to do.

- Splash water on the face before meditating — and even during the day — as a simple but much underrated method of refreshing your energy levels. Atomized water is a great refresher when meditating in a hot environment.
- If you are meditating as part of a group, be relaxed and don't feel embarrassed about moving or shifting if cramping sets in. Meeting with a handful of other meditators can create group chemistry which helps to give your meditation practice a boost.

THE PREPARATION

WHERE TO MEDITATE

When starting with your meditation for the first time, it is normally best to find a quiet spot away from people or animals, where you are not going to be distracted by the telephone, children, visitors, and so on. If you are within hearing distance of a phone and it does ring, allow it to go unanswered or let an answering machine take the call. Half-heard voices or sounds from a television going in the background is a particularly bad distraction, as the mind naturally strains to hear or tries to work out what is being said.

You are unlikely to have the luxury of being able to set aside an entire room purely for the purposes of meditation, but simply a corner will suffice; it is best to make this your regular spot as it will build up its own ambience.

You can turn your quiet corner into a special place using flowers, aromatherapy oils, or perhaps a beautiful object that touches your heart. The emotional response that such items of beauty evoke within you are known to help you enter the alpha mind state more quickly.

Make sure that you can seat yourself very comfortably in your corner.

If the area you have selected is short on space or you are easily distracted by things in the room, you could try the Zen method of facing a

screen or wall with your face about 80cm (30in) away from the surface. The idea is to keep the eyes open throughout the meditation, focusing on the wall or screen. It is a difficult one for most people to do, however it can be good for those who tend to fall asleep during their meditation.

Weather permitting, patios, verandahs and gardens are good places in which to meditate if they are quiet and you are able to remain undistracted by the beauty outdoors. It can be nice to use these areas as a special treat now and again. Changing your place of meditation like this can be quite inspirational, and can act as an energy boost when you are tired or feeling down.

Your decision to try meditation may sometimes confuse the people close to you if they don't know much about it. Put them at ease by explaining to them exactly what you are doing and why you feel you need this quiet time alone; you can also invite them to join you in meditation. If they still don't understand and continue questioning it, remember that you have made a special effort to gain this time so don't be afraid to own it and command it as you have set out to do.

Above **By rearranging the 'junk' in an attic, it is possible to create a special meditation corner for yourself.**

How long to meditate?

As a beginner to meditation, the duration of your initial sessions will be determined by the length of time you are able to concentrate for an uninterrupted period. It is better to meditate for only as long as you feel comfortable — this may be 10 to 15 minutes at first for some people — and build up slowly to 45 minutes as your concentration improves.

The purpose is not to analyze or aim for any goal, as expectations set you up to anticipate a specific result. You need to simply keep a keen but relaxed mindfulness, an awareness of the senses.

When we are completely absorbed in the present we feel joy, peace, security, unity, harmony, sacredness and a vibrant sense of aliveness. These are moments which make life worth living, when we connect with a higher Self. They are moments of wholeness — or holy moments.

— Adapted from Abraham Maslow

TIPS

Keep away from computer monitors and other electrical appliances as they often give out subliminal noise or radiation that interferes with your personal energy vibrations and can subtly disturb the mind.

• Keep a glass of water, tissues, and so on (only the essentials) close at hand so you don't have to keep jumping up.

• Even though you seek out a quiet spot without distraction, the sounds that you may still hear are not to be seen as problems (unless debilitating, of course). Once you are seated, you should acknowledge but not dwell on the sounds you do hear.

Right It can be quite stimulating to take your meditation practice outdoors. A change of scenery will often inspire you and improve your session.

CLOTHING

THERE are no dress codes when it comes to suitable clothing for meditation. The important thing is that your clothes are unstructured, loose-fitting and nonrestrictive.

Of course, at the other end of the spectrum, among Eastern traditions there are certain Yogis who have worn nothing at all — out of poverty, asceticism, to be closer to primordial Nature or even as a mark of achievement! Some Tibetan yogis are known to practise in subzero temperatures. Ultimately though, the idea is to be as comfortable as possible.

Gym gear is also becoming popular in meditation halls, today, although tight-fitting, elasticized gear is not the most ideal for legs that are crossed for an extended period. The legs can also slip off each other if you choose to sit in a lotus position because of the smooth-textured fabrics. However, there are no rules!

It is wise to dress slightly warmer as body temperature drops during meditation, and being cold can become uncomfortable and distracting. Being too warm, on the other hand, can put you to sleep. A large shawl or blanket is an invaluable aid to keep close at hand. This can be used either to keep you warm, to put on the ground under your cushion if the floor is hard or to boost a too-thin cushion.

Some meditators find it helpful to wear a special shawl or item of clothing whose emotional value can inspire their meditational practice. This becomes a symbol of your inner connection and your commitment to what you are doing.

When meditating with a group, it is better not to wear strong perfume as this can be distracting to people around you.

Left **Meditation slows down your circulation, so keep a shawl handy for warmth.**

Seating

This is possibly the most important item of meditating equipment as it has the power to make or break your practice. If, while meditating on your cushion, you are faced with nothing but your unruly mind and numbness or stiffness in the butt, you will not make much progress, so it is wise to get as comfortable and relaxed as you can from the start.

There is a story about a famous Tibetan Yogi, Milarepa, who when once asked by a close disciple for a teaching, in response turned and lifted his robe to expose his very callused rear. Recognizing the immense dedication of his master to his meditation practice, the disciple broke down and wept.

You can use as many cushions as you like for sitting on, bolstering your spine and supporting your legs.

Generally a square shape that offers firm support, such as a polyurethane foam filling, is the most comfortable. If you opt to sit cross-legged on the floor but are a little stiff, raise your hips by sitting on up to four relatively flat cushions. This eases any aches in the knees and hip joints. At any time, your hips should be raised so that they are at a slightly higher level than the knees. This is a good way to ensure you have a straight spine.

Another position favoured by some meditators is to pile cushions one on top of the other so that when you are seated, your knees and shins are placed flat on the floor to either side. This is very good for lengthening the spine.

Buddhists prefer the more traditional *zafu*, a circular cushion of Zen descent, and a *zabuton*, a mat that looks like a small and flat futon. These used to be black but today come in all colours and sizes.

For those wishing to use alternative seating, a stool or straight-backed chair is equally good. It is helpful to select a chair where the height enables you to place the soles of your feet flat on the ground with your thighs parallel to the floor.

Above There are no rules as to what type of cushion you should use — and how many; the most important is to be seated comfortably.

Below Maintaining an upright back in meditation is essential. A supportive chair can help you achieve this.

Meditation postures

Seated postures

Centuries ago, masters of meditation put forward that certain postures enhanced the process of meditation by allowing an unhindered flow of subtle energy between chakras via the meridians and nadis, and around the body (see p57). The breath, too, has a clear passage to flow unhindered to the lungs. On a more practical level, a supported, straight spine above which the head is balanced and relaxed promotes an open and receptive posture that helps you gain control of your mind. You gently breathe out the tensions, aches and pains in your body, so that the mind is not distracted.

The most popular of the meditational postures is the lotus position, followed by the half lotus. Many Eastern meditative traditions describe the meditator's path as a 'warrior' path because it is not easy to meditate with any regularity. The significance of the yogic meditation posture is that it not only supports the neck, back and shoulders but also helps to instil a proud, uplifting attitude in the mind, reinforcing the notion that it takes a certain amount of positiveness, confidence and commitment to look deeply into your own mind.

The most important thing, however, is to be fully comfortable. Not everyone is able to achieve these yogic postures, and loosely crossing or folding the legs in front of you is equally acceptable. Many people find it helps to use the wall as support for the back. Sit on a cushion, with an additional cushion supporting the back, legs extended. Others prefer to sit on a straight-backed chair or a 'prayer stool'. The most essential aspect is to keep the back straight.

In a seated position your buttocks and legs should be comfortable so as not to lead to serious stiffness or cramps (although this is quite normal in the beginning). The chest is very slightly pushed forward, ensuring that the lumbar region is straight and not curved (this can be achieved by drawing the shoulder blades back and gently down). Shoulders should also be down and relaxed. The hands can lie palms face-down on the knees, loosely resting in the lap, or in the meditation *mudra* in the lap. (The Sanskrit word 'mudra' translates as 'sign' or 'token'.) The head is kept erect with the chin tucked in slightly so that the neck maintains the straight line of the vertebrae.

Generally, people prefer to close their eyes during meditation, as it aids concentration and their visualization abilities. The benefit of open-eyed meditation, though, is that it helps train you to maintain a meditative attitude in your daily activities. It enhances your awareness of being grounded in the 'here and now'. If you do keep your eyes open, direct them downwards toward a point 2m (6ft) or so in front of you, though not focusing on anything in particular.

After a little practice you will find that you automatically assume the correct meditation posture. It may seem like the posture calls for rigidity, but you are simply arranging your skeletal structure in such a way that the muscles can relax around them and you have an unimpeded flow of energy. Similarly, the concentration exercises create an environment within, in which the mind can eventually relax. Note the balance: peaceful and relaxed but alert and aware.

Left **The yogic half lotus is favoured as a meditation posture because it is so supportive for the spine.**

Touching the Earth:
The hand rests on top of the knees while kneeling. Significance: it invokes the Earth as a witness to your living with wisdom.

Receptivity:
You are seated cross-legged with the palms facing upward. Significance: you are remaining open to whatever unfolds.

Meditation:
One hand rests on top of the other, fingers overlapping. Significance: calmness and stillness are contributing to steadfastness of mind.

Interconnection:
Thumb and forefinger are touching. Significance: everything relates and connects with everything else; this symbolizes the unity of all things.

Prayer:
The palms and fingers are aligned together. Significance: you are paying tribute to the vast presence of life that is so much greater than your personal existence.

Touching the Elements:
This is a reclining posture with the palms facing up. Significance: to feel moment to moment your connection with the elements of earth, water, fire and air.

MEDITATION POSTURES

LYING OR RECLINING POSTURE

This traditional posture tends to encourage falling asleep. However, it is a good meditation posture to assume in bed when you are struggling to sleep as the result of an active mind despite your physical tiredness.

Lie on the right side of the body (this also aids digestion if you have food in your stomach) with the left leg on top of the right and your head resting on the right palm (bent forearm and elbow on the floor). Legs are stretched straight out, the lower one maintaining good contact with the floor.

An alternative option is to have the knees bent and the heels drawn towards the buttocks.

Above Although you need to be careful not to drift off to sleep in this reclining posture, it gives you a grounding feeling of contact with the earth. It is also a good posture if you are experiencing pain anywhere in your body.

YOUR MEDITATING COMPANIONS

As with starting anything new, it is good to have a peer group of similar-minded people with whom you can share ideas, experiences, and so on. A meditation group is a great way to get quality training and also plays a support role for your new endeavour. Besides valuable contact with various teachers and instructors, these groups usually also offer book, tape and video libraries with a wealth of information for you to further your search. The teachers are normally experts in their field and a great repository of free information. Having, through introspection, 'worked on themselves' for many years, they also usually make great role models for children and adults alike.

To get the best results, most meditation schools encourage a balance between solitary and group meditation. A community of meditators can act as a reflection of your own personal experience, and this often emphasizes how important the community aspect is in terms of healthy interaction and sharing common experiences.

STANDING AND WALKING POSTURES

The basic technique described on the previous pages applies to walking or standing meditation and, for the most part, any other type of meditation such as breathing, mantra chants, and visualizations.

For the walking meditation, the upper half of the body is held in the same way as for sitting meditation but the hands can be held in the 'shielded fist' position, which is common to the martial arts — the left hand covers the right fist at waist level. You should move your legs in such a way that you are not moving so slowly it puts you in a dreamy state or trance, and not so fast as to be distracting or disturbing (see also p51).

Above **Meditation *mudras* vary and are up to the individual, but essentially they honour the sacredness of your practice.**

Above **Beginners benefit greatly from participation in a group meditation, especially if it is led by an experienced teacher.**

IN *all activities of life from trivial to important, the secret of efficiency lies in an ability to combine two seemingly incompatible states — a state of maximum activity and a state of maximum relaxation.*

— Aldous Huxley

AT *some stages you will experience a plateau — as if everything had stopped. This is a hard point in the journey. Know that once the process has started it doesn't stop; it only appears to stop from where you are looking.*

— Ram Dass

BE *gentle with yourself. If you will not be your own unconditional friend, who will be? If you are playing an opponent and you are also opposing yourself — you are going to be outnumbered.*

— Dan Millman

BEGINNER'S MEDITATIONS

HOW TO RELAX

STRETCHING EXERCISE

This is intended as an intermediary exercise to bridge the energies of a normal, frenzied day with the quieter, more introspective energies of meditation. It serves to prepare you for the calmness and stillness that is to follow.

Lie on your back on the floor in your meditation area in a relaxed pose — legs and arms outstretched in a position that is comfortable for you. You are going to stretch every extremity of your body from head to toe. As you tense, then release, the different parts of your body, imagine all the tension that has built up during the day releasing with the relaxing of the muscles.

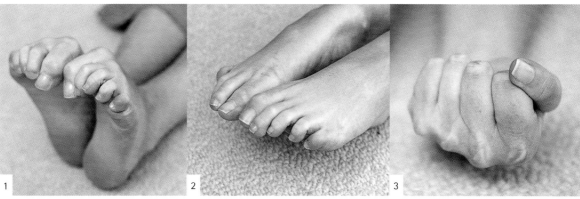

Starting with your feet, wriggle your toes to locate and feel them, then squeeze them together (1) on each foot. Hold, then relax on an outbreath. Point your toes forward, feeling the stretch in the arch, hold, then flex them up, feeling the stretch in the Achilles tendon at the back of your heel. Relax while breathing out.

Moving up to the calves, stretch out your legs through the toes (2), pulling up your kneecaps and feel the calves tightening. Hold, and relax on an outbreath. Tense up the thigh muscles and hold, before releasing. Move to the buttocks, clenching them tightly, then relax. Next come the stomach muscles, then the chest muscles.

Move to your arms, stretching them downward away from your shoulders, as far along the carpet or floor as you can. Tense them so that the elbows lift slightly from the floor. Relax. Clench your fists (3), then release.

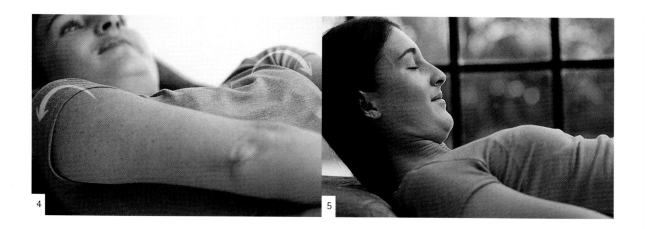

Roll your shoulders back (4), move your shoulder blades together and down your back, at the same pushing out your sternum to open up your chest. Breathe deeply.

Clench your jaw and tense your neck muscles, then release. Gently raise your head forward to lengthen the back of the neck (5), then lower back to the floor.

Work the muscles of your face by scrunching the eyes (6), pulling the lips into a smile, then grimace, and relax. Visualize your ears and head tightening, then releasing.

Imagine all your tension flowing out of the top of your head. At this point, you should be physically relaxed and ready to begin with your meditation.

A NOTE ON RELAXATION

It is important not to mix up relaxation with the practice of meditation. Essentially, they complement each other, but you cannot meditate successfully until your body is completely relaxed because your attention is diverted to your areas of tension. In the same way, the most beneficial relaxation comes through focused awareness. Dreaming, 'tuning out', or even going into a trance will not produce the same results as opening up your awareness while allowing your muscles and body to release their tension, area by area, muscle by muscle. These aspects eventually come together on their own through meditation, and you quite naturally and without effort become *aware* during your relaxation time and *relaxed* during meditation.

AS discussed earlier, relaxation needs to be integrated skilfully into your life for you to live fully and with enjoyment. You create equilibrium if you maintain an awareness of each present moment and a sense of ease with your inner self.

As a beginner it is a good idea to start all relaxation and meditation exercises with the stretching session featured on pp38–39, simply to prepare your body and mind for the period of stillness to come.

These three relaxation exercises are excellent for removing all traces of tension in body, mind and spirit. As you do in meditation, you need to carry out these exercises slowly and with care; it is time well spent and is good for personal growth. The Pine Mist and Shining Star practices can be done in a quiet space during lunchtime or in your office, behind a closed door, if you need to re-energize at any time during the day.

Whatever idea people may have about positive thinking and visualization, studies have shown that it works even for people who are unsure about its effects. Feel free to enhance these practices at home by creating your own special atmosphere using incense, candles, aromatherapy oils, or even crystals to help you relax more deeply and enhance your self-awareness.

SPARKLING LIQUID

This is not only an excellent practice for removing tensions locked in the muscles of the body, but is also good to prepare you for sleep — in fact, it is often very difficult to remain awake during this process. It is best to lie flat and do a minute or so of slow and deep breathing,. Start by concentrating on the toes, physically feeling them, then relaxing them completely. Imagine the enzymes responsible for maintaining the rigidity of your muscles dissolving through your pores. Mentally move on to the feet, ankles, calves and so forth, up your body to the crown of your head. Take your time, and move slowly and deliberately. By the time you have reached the top of your head, you should be well relaxed. Now imagine a clear, sparkling liquid washing over your skin and cleansing any residual chemicals and tightness away, leaving you relaxed and refreshed.

SHINING STAR

This relaxation practice is good for stress arising from inner confusion or a troubled mind. Again, any comfortable position is good — especially a sitting one. Once more, take a moment of quietness with several deep breaths. Then visualize an intensely bright white light just a foot above your head like your own tiny star. Allow your body, mind and spirit, all the negatives and the positives in your head, to take on the energy of this light and become quiescent like light itself. This should leave you feeling relaxed, positive and peaceful.

Above and left Mental visualization is a highly successful method of introducing the novice to ways of training the mind. By harnessing the compelling energy of the imagination, people are able to transport themselves to other levels of consciousness, thus removing themselves from the potential drudgery of their daily existence. Through the inspiring and uplifting nature of imagination, a person can be motivated to make very positive changes to their lives via the mind, will and intent.

PINE MIST

This practice is good for the energy-depleting effects of destructive worries and inner arguments on the body. Relax in a comfortable position. After a short period of quietness and a few deep breaths, visualize breathing a glowing pine mist (or steam if you are in a cold environment) into your lungs, then imagine it permeating the rest of the body, dissolving all the negativity in your whole being. Visualize this mist cleaning and invigorating your body's entire energy network, leaving you feeling relaxed and energized.

MINDFULNESS VS AWARENESS

THERE are two approaches to meditation — these are mindfulness and awareness. Mindfulness meditation has as its main objectives a state of peace, tranquillity and calmness of the mind, which learns to rest in its inherent state of clarity at the same time being fully aware in the moment.

The intent of awareness meditation is to explore and gain insight into the mind. This insight comes only once calm and clarity have been achieved — awareness is therefore only possible after mindfulness.

Either of the two approaches is always present in any type of meditation, whether it is the centring prayer of the Christian faith or the quiet breathing meditation of someone focusing to de-stress.

MINDFULNESS

In training you to be acutely conscious of the present moment, mindfulness meditation directs you to concentrate singlepointedly on a 'support', which can be any beautiful object, from a stone, statue or crystal to a mantra or the breath. Essentially, the role of the support is that it helps to hold your attention.

Before you start to meditate, it is good to focus on your breathing. Take three deep breaths of air (these are often referred to as the 'three centring breaths'), filling first the bottom of the lungs, then the centre, and finally the top third, before breathing out regularly and slowly. You are engaging in abdominal breathing — drawing air in from the base of the rib cage rather than the upper lungs; you can feel your diaphragm expand outwards as you inhale.

This breathing assists easy posture because you are naturally aligning your spine, helps focus your attention, and induces a state of calm since you are breathing slightly deeper than normal.

DEVICE VS SUPPORT IN MEDITATION

Essentially you are trying to achieve a clear mind that is devoid of thoughts, although only the most experienced of meditators find eventual success in getting their thoughts to cease. A mind that has created space within and thus has reached its inherent state of clarity is the most powerful.

SUPPORT

The use of a support serves to remind you to reign in the mind as soon as you realize it has wandered. It is not possible to completely cut out all thinking, so beginners should take heart. The aim is to be able to turn away from them; by not engaging in them, they will dissolve and disappear. However, obsessive thoughts *will* keep intruding into your mind space. The use of a support is invaluable here. By changing your focus to it, your attention is diverted from compulsive thoughts and taken up by the support.

DEVICE

This may be an easier meditation for beginners to start with because you are being given something to 'do': a mantra to repeat, an object to concentrate on. You make use of the device to prevent the mind from wandering by engaging it to focus on only one thing — the passage of breath, the vibrations of a mantra, or the contours of a treasured item. It is, however, as powerful a form of meditation as any.

Above right Like the steam from a teapot, or breathing out on a frosty morning, the breath only becomes visible with contrasts in temperature. Deceptive though it is, our breath is a powerful tool in times of stress when it can be effectively used to calm the nervous system and clarify thinking.

coaxing the meditator's mind into the deep alpha state. In the Buddhist tradition, meditating on the breath reminds us how the movement of life is mirrored by the breath's endless ebb and flow, reinforcing for us the fact that the only certainty we have in this life is impermanence and change, like the fluctuating rising and falling of the breath.

BREATH MEDITATION

As a Support

Here, the breath is used to generally calm and hone the mind and invite positive energy into your being. In its role as support, the breath acts as a single point of focus for the mind to return to each time you become aware that your thoughts have wandered.

It is better to breathe in through the nose as the fine hair in the nostrils purifies the air, and warms and moistens it for the throat and lungs. Exhale through the nose, too. Focus on the nostrils, concentrating particularly on the feel of the flow of air in and out, in and out. Become an observer, watching its passage as it enters and leaves the nose. Feel the sense of quietness it creates within you.

Then, place your attention on the breath itself and follow its course into the body, and out again. Travel with it into the vast depths, experiencing the breath's soft, regular rhythm. Relax into this rhythm and feel the peace infuse your entire body.

If your mind drifts off too easily, try counting the breaths: repeatedly count to four, or count sequentially. A Zen method is to count to 10, then repeat. Remember that it can take months before you feel you are mastering this process. Don't try too hard or become angry if you are struggling. Be patient and kind with yourself. The idea is that the 'drifting off' becomes the cue to renew your concentration. Eventually you will find that you can still your mind without too much of a struggle.

THE IMPORTANCE OF BREATH

The breath is our life-force; it keeps us alive. By bringing oxygen into our lungs and from there infusing every cell of the body, our systems and organs are replenished and revitalized. It not only sustains us physically; our thoughts, emotions, beliefs and subtle energy systems are also supported by the breath. Because of this powerful link, the act of breathing can be used as a pacifying influence on anxiety, panic and fear. It is very important for people to realize that in a panic-stricken situation, when they react with controlled, slow, deep breathing, this will calm the nervous system, lower the heart rate and lead to clearer thinking.

The breath also has a direct relation to our sense of vitality, and can enhance or deplete our energy reserves depending on whether we're engaged in shallow, superficial breathing or full, deep, nourishing breathing.

The breath, therefore, plays a crucial role in meditation, first by centring and relaxing the meditator thus introducing a sense of stillness to his or her practice, then by acting as a focal point on which the mind can concentrate instead of wandering, and finally, through the resulting stillness, by

As a Device

This meditation teaches you to use the breath as part of a visualization technique to stimulate and rejuvenate your energy. It has a positive and uplifting effect on mind and body, subtly enhancing longevity.

Sitting in the normal meditation posture, focus firstly on the in-breath coming through your nose. Imagine the breath either as intense white light or as a vibrant stream in the colours of the rainbow. Feel this radiant light being drawn into your being, fully cleaning and rejuvenating your mind and body. Visualize all the negativity and lack of energy being carried out on the out-breath, leaving you feeling cleansed and peaceful.

Below Traditionally, violet is associated with spirituality, and indigo with intuition, which is why amethyst can be a useful accessory for meditation.

TIPS

To handle the constant flow of thoughts, try to be aware of:
- The first thought or image as it arises so you can bring your mind back to the breath before it is distracted by others crowding in.
- Your emotions as they come up; simply be aware of them, letting them rise and fall like a wave. If they are powerful and persist, they may need to be cleared separately.

In trying to turn away from your thoughts, focus on the following:
- Remind yourself that thoughts remain as such unless you act upon them.
- Visualize the thought passing on. Imagine you are beside a river, then drop your thoughts into the flowing waters and watch them float away. Be aware of the space between the letting go of one thought and the arising of the next one. There is a saying: 'Meditation starts in the space between the thoughts.'

VISUAL IMAGE MEDITATION

As a Support

An interesting stone, beautifully shaped or textured piece of wood, special picture, statue of a god or image of a master all appeal to your sense of vision. Here, you should take *note* of what you are seeing but you do not *think* about it or have an internal discussion in your mind. The 'awareness' faculty of your brain can note the details of the object, but there should be no mental engaging or activity occurring. It is important to get beyond the inquisitive nature of the mind which continually seeks novelty and distraction.

Bring your focus back to the object whenever you find your mind has become distracted by thoughts.

As a Device

Although any of the above objects would be suitable, a crystal is used as an example here. This technique makes use of as many of the senses as possible, especially visualization. Place the crystal of choice on the floor, some distance from where you are seated. After quieting yourself, focus on its colour, its clarity or cloudiness, its shape, how many facets it has, whether it is rough or polished. Think

about its weight, how it would feel in the palm of your hand, whether it feels warm or cold. Then see what associations you make between its colour and, say, similar colours of Nature; perhaps its hue reminds you of a flower or golden wheatfields or a damp green forest. If so, then think of the smell this evokes. Be aware of the emotions that are linked to these associations. When you are ready, allow the visualizatons to fade and bring yourself slowly to the present.

Right The five elements exist in most Eastern traditions, although their specific properties tend to differ — Hindu-derived wisdom talks of earth, water, fire, air and ether, whereas Chinese tradition replaces the latter two elements with metal and wood. However, in each case all elements relate to colour, the emotions and the five senses. In meditation, the presence of one or more of the five elements serves to reinforce our oneness with Nature and the universe.

MANDALAS

SOME objects used in meditation contain a deeper meaning or significance which can enhance the benefit of your meditation. For example, statues and deity images are not only objects of devotion but also contain symbolism in their poses and gestures. By allowing this symbolism to become part of your subconscious, it can help you absorb their meaning.

Likewise, the intricate designs of mandalas and the sacred geometry of yantras symbolize the world as cyclic and ordered in nature.

The mandala (the most well known are from the Hindu and Buddhist cultures) is made up of various intricate designs, usually circular in shape, which represent wholeness and unity — wholeness of the self, the unity of

Left As part of a traditional ceremony, **Tibetan Buddhists kneel over a period of several weeks to create, with meticulous care, a giant sand mandala. This they do using their mouths to gently lay intricate, jewel-coloured designs with the aid of straws. There is absolute mindfulness in the work because the joy is in its creation. The process requires complete detachment, however, as once it is complete, it is swept away with a broom. The lesson: the impermanence of life.**

life, and the oneness of all things in the Universe. The mandala is a diagrammatically symbolic example of a mind in its perfected, absolute state: the enlightened mind. By focusing on a mandala you stimulate the source of universal energy within yourself, which brings about the healing of mind and body. It also represents the ebb and flow of the cycles of life, so that by contemplating the mandala you achieve a sense of acceptance and understanding of where you are in a particular life cycle.

Meditating on a yantra (one of many sacred geometric figures, the most common of which represents intersecting triangles) is of more immediate benefit since it is not as complex in configuration as a mandala. One should gaze at the image without being distracted by any of the forms — the automatic inclination is to try to analyze them. The mind needs to simply absorb the image as a whole. Intuition has its way of decoding this 'spiritual map'. In most Eastern traditions the belief is that we are all born enlightened beings but social conditioning obscures this inner wisdom and we eventually ignore or block out our intuitive abilities; our path in life is to bring this inherent state of enlightenment to the fore of the conscious mind.

Sound meditation

As a Support

The use of sound in meditation, particularly inspiring music, serves as an excellent background for visualizations. It also evokes an atmosphere before starting a meditation; music creates a magical space within which meditators find it easier to work. Classical music is uplifting and there is a multitude of New Age Music CDs available for meditation. Many focus on musical instruments that have a certain clarity and purity of sound; they can incorporate the sounds of Nature such as water, rain, the wind, a thunderstorm, and so on. The intention essentially is not to listen, but simply to hear.

As a Device

In this type of meditation, you recognize and acknowledge the sounds as they come to your attention. Hear each sound but don't consciously listen or wait for the next one, and don't give any of the sounds a specific importance. The sound also serves as a helpful reminder to bring the mind back to it as a support every time it starts to wander off. It is the meditation that's important; the sound is simply the support object. If it is more than that, it is a distraction.

This page **Focusing on sound in meditation helps a beginner's concentration, and prevents the mind from wandering.**

There is a story about a monk who survived the infamous torture method of constant, dripping water without any ill effect. He was questioned later about how he managed to cope with this gruelling ordeal. He replied that for him every drop was neither the first, last nor one of a string of drops, but that each drop was the only drop. Since his mind was focused in the present, that one drop was the only drop that existed for him at any one point; with the next drop it was

the same. Similarly, you should try to notice sounds only as they occur. Nothing preceding or following a sound exists in that precise moment.

UNDERSTANDING THE MANTRA

Physicists were perplexed to discover about 90 years ago that the material world, instead of being composed of 'building blocks' of physical matter, in actual fact was formed by a dance of energy — the result of myriad oscillating atomic particles held together by an underlying creative vibration. This vibration maintains the pattern of interrelationships between these energies, so forming matter. This 'new' scientific knowledge was already

Below Invocations (often Om Mani Padme Hum — see Sanskrit, centre) on Buddhist prayer flags are released to God with each wind-blown flutter.

known to all the ancient systems of wisdom in both East and West, who referred to this primal energy from which all is formed with names such as the 'audible life stream' and the 'voice of the silence'. Perhaps the best known is the Sanskrit term 'Om'.

In ancient traditions, sounds were used to heal people physically, energetically or spiritually. Because these sounds vibrate with a higher energy, they tap into a person's consciousness and align it with their higher, spiritual self, literally changing their consciousness (hence, 'sacred sounds').

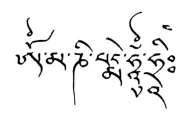

USING A MANTRA

A mantra is a sacred sound, and can be used by you to imbue yourself with

an attribute from this underlying ocean of energy that is behind all physical and subtle matter. Used in the form of a sound, word, phrase or sentence, the mantra is either breathed silently, whispered, sung, chanted or, simply, spoken. It is a basic meditating tool and is used in nearly every path that practises meditation. A repeated 'Hail Mary' in the Catholic tradition is as much a mantra as 'Om' for the Buddhist in Tibet.

The advantage of using a mantra is that the sound can hold your concentration more easily than any other focus. The human voice is regarded as the most powerful instrument for carrying sacred energy; a mantra is therefore a powerful way of accelerating your growth.

Besides the psychological effect of repeating a word containing a specific meaning over and over (you wouldn't be unaffected if you spoke a word for Peace a few hundred times), it calms

and balances you, takes you beyond the chatter of the mind, gives you mental clarity, and bathes you in the quality inherent in the meaning of the words. Because the sound of the voice is resonating through you, over time you start to absorb and express the quality of that mantra.

Mantras in ancient languages are more commonly used because it is said that in the past people were closer to 'the Source', therefore these languages held more spiritual power. Perhaps what is more important is the sincerity, desire and intention behind the words and the clarity with which you repeat them. Some meditation traditions say the mantra only 101 or 109 times, using beads to keep tally on the number of times the words have been spoken, then follow the speaking with a silent meditation that rests in the resonance of the sound. Other schools repeat the mantra for the full duration of the meditation.

In choosing a mantra, it is helpful to select a word whose quality you feel you personally need to develop. For instance, if you were feeling a lack of either creativity, courage, peace, patience or compassion, you could precede the word of your choice with 'I Am ...', or 'I Am Divine ...'; it would contain the power of that quality. One of the best known mantras, Om Mani Padme Hum ('the jewel in the heart of the lotus'), has the effect of increasing compassion in you, to protect you and align you with your inner spiritual being.

The syllable OM, which is the imperishable Brahman, is the universe. Whatsoever has existed, whatsoever exists, whatsoever shall exist hereafter, is OM. And whatsoever transcends past, present and future, that is also OM.

— **Mandukya Upanishad**

Through the sounding of the word OM (AUM) and through reflection of its meaning, the Way is found. From this comes the realization of the Inner Self and the removal of all obstacles.

— Patanjali's **Yoga Sutra**

CLOSING YOUR MEDITATION

A meditation session can also be closed with Om. Its aptness lies in the belief that it is the 'sound from which all sound originates' — that 'white sound' quality that underlies the silence of Nature such as the whisper of a breeze or the imperceptible rustle of grass. When you repeat the Om sound, the vibration it sets up in your body allows you to tune into the vibrations of your environment around you, helping you feel your connectedness with all living things of the Universe. Inhale through your nose and on a long exhalation, vocalize the 'om' sound slowly, extending your exhalation as long as possible.

Above **The mantra Om used by Buddhists has three distinct sounds — ahh, uhh, mmm — hence the spelling Aum.**

WALKING MEDITATION

This meditation focuses on the sense of touch, where one's mindfulness is directed to the soles of the feet and the sensation of their contact with the ground. Doing this barefoot allows you to properly feel the textures underneath the foot, although wearing socks on flooring or a carpet is also quite acceptable.

Hold the head straight, eyes looking slightly down. Keep the hands together at the waistline, one hand on the abdomen with the other placed on top, to allow you to remain focused on the feet. Concentrate on the feeling as the foot touches the ground — the contact, then the pressure caused by your shifting body weight, and finally the relaxation as the pressure eases. Focus also on the texture underfoot and the warmth or coldness (if you are outdoors or perhaps barefoot indoors). Maintain a very, very slow pace.

You can also synchronize your breathing with your steps; for example, inhale for three steps, exhale for the next three. Or you could take more steps on the inhalation and fewer on the exhalation, or vice versa.

You could choose to walk up and down the same stretch, walk around in a circle (normally clockwise to follow the cycle of the Universe) or meander along a path. Agitated office workers needing to calm themselves before a tense meeting or as a result of a heated altercation can do this during their lunchtime break.

Walking meditation can very easily be incorporated into your daily activities — for instance, while walking to the car, between appointments, or even around the home.

It is also a good way of breaking up your sitting practice-sessions to re-energize and refocus the mind and body (it need only be a short spell).

Below **A walking meditation is all about being mindful of the sensations underfoot, but this is enhanced when you create an atmosphere for yourself.**

AWARENESS MEDITATION

In this form of meditation you don't concentrate on anything at all, but rest the mind in the simple awareness of itself — in an effort eventually to learn to understand your natural mind state. Mindfulness teaches you to be fully aware in the presence of the moment; awareness opens up and expands the quality of that sense of knowing. In reality, of course, your thoughts come up and distract you. Initially, concentrate on acknowledging these distractions as they come up, but try not to engage in any of them. The effort lies in the experiencing of being in the present with your senses awakened but not thinking about the experience. This is a much harder type of meditation, and is generally easier to approach after having practised mindfulness.

AN EXERCISE IN AWARENESS

This particular meditation exercise is technically a mixture of both mindfulness and awareness (or insight) meditation but the ultimate aim is to rest in a clear, quiescent awareness. It is a little more difficult — it is one of the more advanced and powerful meditations as it leads very quickly and directly to the mind's true nature. If you could plan to do only half an hour a day of this meditation for a few years, the benefits would be quite formidable. It is also possible to do this meditation in the office, at your desk during work hours, if you have the need to remove yourself from the hustle and bustle of a stressful day.

Sitting comfortably, start to focus your attention on the breath, but only the out-breath. This focused attention brings you constantly back to being in the present. Become aware of the breath going out, then let the noticing of it trail away so that there has been a gap in your concentration when you breathe in. Although this gap or space in your mental workings seems like nothing at all, it is actually the truest state of the mind and this is what we try to encourage through meditation. It is this 'empty' state of mind that all accomplished meditators learn to discover. When cultivated, it leads to a fuller and more harmonious life.

Left Be assured, you will get to a point where you can focus inwards quietly at your desk and feel quite refreshed afterward.

Grounding yourself

It is always a good thing to end off any meditation session with a grounding routine to reinforce the union of the mental and spiritual with the physical body, and to re-establish your connectedness with the Earth.

Earth energy

Visualize in your mind's eye how you perceive the earth's energy – it could be fiery lava, bubbling liquid mud, molten crystal, or a deep red glow (reflecting the colour of the base chakra which is your connection with the earth).

Then imagine that you are penetrating deep into the earth, through layer upon layer of soil, rock, water, minerals. The deeper you go, the more malleable the layers become and the warmer the temperature. Imagine that you are approaching the fiery centre of turbulent molten lava, then draw this earth energy into every fibre of your body, breathing it into your pores.

Eventually you slowly return to the surface of the earth, feeling your oneness with it and a sense of being solidly grounded and balanced.

Obstacles and traps

Problems that arise during meditation are often called 'obstacles'. These are blocks to your progress, especially noticeable when you have been particularly busy or you are overtired, and you are having difficulty getting past distractions or even settling down for a meditation.

Meditation's cyclic nature

Be aware that at times your meditation sessions will be a wonderful experience, at others you will feel that you are making little or no progress, even regressing! Each meditation is different because you are affected by the complex cycle of energies within you and in the world around you – for example, changing seasons and weather, your personal biorhythms, even your moods will affect your meditation experience. Because of this, there may be times when you struggle to make or maintain an inner connection during meditation. Relax and don't force, strain or try too hard. Don't judge yourself. It is absolutely fine to leave the meditation for a while. You may find that when you do return, you will make a deeper connection.

Take heart! Be assured that at some stage you will reach a point where every meditation is worthwhile regardless of what you are going through in your daily life, and the good sessions will become even better.

Control

Some of us are 'control addicts' and are too afraid to let go and release ourselves fully into the experience. By holding back, you are not allowing yourself to open, grow and change. You cannot go wrong by submitting to your higher self for it is the true centre of your being.

Your rational mind

The analyzing, judging mind is a major obstacle to sustained and deep meditation because it divides the physical world from the spiritual. The minute rationality and judgement are applied to your meditation experience, you lose your focus. Allow the mind to stand aside, let go of any expectations and simply trust the process.

Denying emotions

Some people feel that if they meditate they won't need to deal with their emotional baggage. But to become whole, you need to honour your emotions and they can only be handled or cleared by engaging with them (see Clearing Emotions, p66).

The feelings of your truest self – love, peace, serenity – can only emerge once you have cleared the emotional blockages. The more you can engage with your feelings and clear any negative patterns, the more profound and rewarding your meditation will be.

YOU are in physical existence to learn and understand that your energy, translated into feelings, thoughts and emotions, causes all experience. There are no exceptions.

— Seth

LOVE it the way it is! The way you see the world depends entirely on your own vibration. When your vibration changes the whole world will look different. It's like those days when everyone seems smiling at you because you feel happy.

— Thaddeus Golas

PERCEPTION is a mirror, not a fact. And what I look on is my state of mind, reflected outward.

— A Course in Miracles

EMPOWERING YOURSELF

YOU ARE ENERGY

MEDITATION *teaches us to tap into our powerful mental and spiritual energies, and it helps to understand that we are energetic, vibrational beings, not just solid matter — which is the generally held perception.*

Science has shown the body's physical mass to consist of between 75 and 80 per cent water, in which are widely spaced atoms held together by electromagnetic forces. The bonding structure of this water can be affected by the transmitting of energy through the body, which is why we have such powerful abilities to set into motion our own healing potential. We are, in actual fact, 80 to 90 per cent vibrational beings. What we see as matter, therefore (including the natural world around us — animals, trees, plants, inanimate objects of Nature) is actually energy — or light — which vibrates at different frequencies. These frequencies resonate with the countless vibrations emanating from the living, breathing environment around us.

The human body is surrounded by an energetic shield, called the aura, which itself consists of a series of energy fields — known in metaphysical terms as the subtle bodies. They serve to align the soul — or spirit — with the physical world. The energy layer closest to the physical body is known as the physical aura or etheric double.

This human energy system is extremely complex and intricate, with interacting and overlapping fields of subtle energy vibrating at their own frequencies which, although invisible to the human eye, range from dense to the finest of substances. Those nearest to the physical body are the most dense. Within these many layers of subtle energies are the chakras. Although Chakra is a Sanskrit word meaning 'circle' or 'wheel', it is also common in Native American cultures and Hebrew kabbalism. These are actually vortices of energy which both radiate and draw in universal energy and without which we would not be able to have a physical body or function in a physical world. Another way of describing them is that they are transformers of energy from one dimension to another.

Although each of our subtle energy fields holds its own level of chakras, traditionally we work with those in the etheric body, which is the energetic blueprint of each individual's physical vehicle in the subtle spheres. The major chakras are more or less in line in front of the spine. The chakras create the aura and determine the condition of thoughts and feelings, and the degree to which organs are functioning. Any imbalances distort the auric energy field. Blockages or interference in the full functioning of a chakra will show up in the aura as a dense patch of trapped energy or impure colour.

The seven major chakras are in front of the spine (see illustration) and these are the ones we mainly work with, but there are many minor ones in the body and new ones opening up as our consciousness evolves. Each major chakra has a predominant colour but when they are functioning to maximum capacity one chakra might radiate a combination of colours. Therefore it is best to work with the traditionally accepted colour for that chakra.

The functioning of any chakra is dependent on the perceptions and beliefs you hold about yourself and your relationship to others and the world. For instance, if you are lacking self-esteem and you hold a belief that you are not worthy or as competent as others, this will show up as a blockage in your solar plexus chakra. It is the function of this chakra to transform

Chakras	Colour	Position	Related organs/glands	Emotional functions
Base	Red	In front of coccyx	Adrenals, kidneys, colon, rectum	Security, survival, base instinct
Sacral centre	Orange	Above pubic bone	Reproductive systems	Sexual/emotional response, feelings of pleasure
Solar plexus	Yellow	Diaphragm	Pancreas, intestines, liver, spleen	Personal power, self-esteem, mental/emotional control
Heart	Green	Midway of sternum between breasts	Heart, lungs, circulatory system, thymus gland	Love, forgiveness, healing, compassion
Throat	Blue	Throat indentation	Thyroid/parathyroid glands, throat, mouth	Communication, expression, discernment
Brow	Indigo	Between eyebrows	Pituitary gland, brain (partial), eyes, ears	Intuition, insight, psychic abilities
Crown	Violet	Crown	Pineal gland, brain	Gateway to higher consciousness, spirituality

universal energy into your sense of power and your interface with other people and your external world. If you hold the belief that you are a whole, complete human being, living in trust in an intelligent, supportive world which has meaning, and all the areas in your life are functioning in balance and to their fullest potential, then your chakras will, for the most part, be operating to their maximum capacity.

The value of working with your chakra system is that you can monitor personal levels of physical, mental, psychological, and spiritual health. You can activate the chakras by working on them in meditation, and any issues that are causing energy blockages will start to surface from your subconscious mind and, if you are committed to your healing, will give you an opportunity to deal with them. When your chakras are all open and functioning fully, it gives you a wonderful sense of wholeness and empowerment as well as a strong boost of energy.

THE ROLE OF THE CHAKRAS

Although working with chakras is not accepted as part of mainstream medical healthcare, modern science and technology are proving that in the human body, electromagnetic energy pulses at each of the spots corresponding with the seven chakras are stronger than in other areas of the body.

The chakras govern the body's central nervous system and the seven ductless glands responsible for secreting hormones into the bloodstream. Working together with the chakras is a system of 14 energy channels known as meridians. These link up the nerve pathways of the autonomic nervous system (responsible for the body's involuntary functions) and each meridian in turn governs and influences an organ or body system. Located along the meridians are the reflex points used in acupuncture (acupressure).

The power of thought — and the role of positive energy frequencies being able to restore vibrational imbalances — has already been touched on, and this is where the benefits of meditation and mind control can have a major influence.

By focusing on the charged electrical energies that exist between the atoms of the body's cells, cell layers can be physically influenced by transmitting positive thought vibrations to the specific area of the body. The same can be done using colour, crystals and gems, and sounds (see panel).

COLOUR'S PROPERTIES

- **Red:** energizing, stimulating, activating
- **Orange:** revitalizing in a warmer, gentler way; good for energy and vitality
- **Yellow:** purifying, warming, arouses mental activity
- **Green:** balances, harmonizes, regenerates
- **Blue:** cooling, calming, soothing and relaxing
- **Violet:** stimulates mental creativity and inspiration.

Above **This trail of lights at a funfair is reminiscent of the spiralling vortex attributed to the body's seven chakras.**

Use of colour and crystals in meditation and healing

As already discussed, to be in physical, mental and emotional good health the body, its systems and organs need to be in tune with one another. Disease or discord in any area of the body upsets the vibrational rhythm, for each part influences and is affected by other parts, and each is dependent upon the others and the whole. Colour, which is a property of light and therefore has vibrational properties, plays a significant role both in meditation and in healing your physical and subtle energies. Because thoughts too are electrical energy, positive affirmations and intentions can bring about changes to the aura's electrical field — transmitted from the mental level to the etheric subtle body and finally the physical body.

Colour

Scientifically, light is composed of seven major colours, of which three are the primary colours red, yellow and blue — these cannot be produced by mixing colours. Combinations of the primaries make up the balance of the seven major colours.

Colour generally vibrates at the same rate as light, although each colour of the spectrum is the product of a slightly different wave length and vibration frequency. Thus each has its own characteristics and can affect human energies. Those with higher frequency vibrations will stimulate the higher frequencies of the brain; those with a lower frequency can influence the physical body and its systems. These different colour frequencies are used for healing and balancing, and stimulating deeper levels of consciousness.

In the field of energy healing, colour can be applied in any form, whether locked in a crystal or gemstone, distilled in a flower essence, used as coloured lights or via a projector with colour filters. Note how each chakra — as a vortex of electromagnetic energy — spins at its own frequency to produce its individual colour.

This is why in meditation it is a popular practice to use crystals or colour visualization where you breathe the corresponding colour into your chakras or draw bright light into yourself from the sky and the earth.

Crystals

Crystals and gems can be calming and grounding (for example, in meditation) or can stimulate healing of the physical body through their ability to vibrate and resonate. They absorb, store, and transmit energy. When disease in the body creates unstable molecular patterns, a clear quartz crystal can be used to direct and focus light and energy (much in the same way as a laser beam does) onto the area to be healed, bringing it into harmony and balance.

An example of two suitable crystals to use in meditation is lapis lazuli and amethyst. The deep blue of the former relates to both the throat and brow chakras, influencing communication, expression, and creativity. In meditation, it opens deeper levels of consciousness. On a physical level, it is good for headaches and migraines.

The violet of amethyst corresponds with the crown chakra, and stimulates intuition, awakens spirituality, and raises energies to higher frequencies. On a physical level, amethyst is also good for headaches, and insomnia.

A SELECTION OF MEDITATIONS

GROUNDING MEDITATION

THE TREE

This meditation can be done as a visualization but it is even more powerful if you do it while physically leaning against a tree. Remember that plants and trees have their own energy field and that there will be a transfer of energy occurring between you.

If you are seated in your meditation spot (rather than outdoors), imagine that you are sitting with your back against a tree. Slowly meld yourself with the bark of that tree and become it. Imagine its (your) roots penetrating deep into the earth and being nourished, then watch the branches extending into the sky towards the sun's warmth. Feel the solidity of the trunk as the centre of your body. Touch the floor beside you with your hands and imagine that you are feeling the warmth of the earth and your connectedness with it.

The following meditations can be applied to many different areas of your life. If you practise them regularly, they can effect powerful changes to your outlook, attitudes, creativity and energy levels for a greatly enhanced existence.

Begin with a grounding meditation to align your energies with the earth's energies and get you into a calm, still space.

Above **The use of visualization in meditation is an underestimated magical tool which works on fantasy to open a gateway into 'reality' — a reality that exists at the deeper levels of your consciousness. Visualization amplifies that which you are trying to access, and can ultimately take you into higher states of consciousness.**

CREATING YOUR OWN SAFE SPACE

If you are learning to meditate for the first time, a worthwhile exercise is to create a sacred, special place in your mind into which you can retreat at any time. The importance is that it remains constant, that it acts as a protective haven, and evokes positive emotions when you mentally go there. This special place is used for healing, calming, doing inner work and saying positive affirmations.

Your special space could be anything your heart desired and should bring on pleasurable feelings of happiness and contentment: a magical cave, a beautiful garden perfumed with the scent of flowers, a temple on a mountaintop, a pristine powder-sand beach, or even a bubble in outer space. Put into it things that touch you with their beauty, for example, a gorgeous crystal, a splashing waterfall, fish jumping in a pool, or a beautiful animal.

Close your eyes and breathe deeply to still yourself. Imagine yourself in that sacred space, with all your senses heightened. Go around smelling, touching, tasting and feeling everything around you. Make it alive and real. It is a place you can feel completely safe in. You can retreat to this secret place at any time of day, whenever you feel you need to remove yourself briefly from the activity of your life. It takes very little time and effort, but its calming effects are immeasurable.

Right The special space people go to in their head will be different for everyone. It is a place in which they feel perfectly protected and safe.

MEDITATION ON THE CHAKRAS

Seated in your meditation spot, first calm yourself with a few deep, slow breaths and then close your eyes. Place your attention on your root chakra, feel it connected to the earth and imagine energy being transferred from the earth upwards into the base of your body. Focus on the area of the coccyx and as you breathe in, infuse the chakra located there with deep ruby-red light. Visualize it as a shimmering sphere, and concentrate on its size, shape and quality.

As you breathe out, allow the colour to deepen and brighten, and when it is luminous and steady, on an inhalation imagine a thread of white light moving up the spine to connect with the navel chakra.

Exhale, then breathing in, infuse this area with a deep orange and again focus on the qualities of the sphere. When the navel chakra is luminous and steady, take the thread of bright white light up the spine to the solar plexus. Breathe yellow light into this chakra. After each chakra, pause and be aware of all the other coloured spheres glowing equally,

connected by their thread of silver light. Progress slowly and steadily up the spine to the green heart chakra, then to the blue throat chakra, the indigo third eye, and finally, the violet crown chakra. When you get to the crown, pause again and take note of the luminous intensity of each chakra and the cord linking them.

Then imagine clear, protective light emerging from the crown and shimmering around the body and its chakras, flowing down to the ground. See your entire body being held in this protective glow. Finally, let the light fade, and quietly become aware again of your physical body.

A good grounding gesture after opening your eyes is to press your palms into the floor, visualizing any excess energy leaving the hands and penetrating the earth.

Below The roots of the lotus flower, a type of water lily, are attached to the earth below and its bloom opens to the sun above. It is thus an apt Buddhist symbol of enlightenment.

Boosting self-esteem

Self-love meditation

This is a valuable visualization meditation which can be done for 10 minutes daily to build up self-esteem and confidence. It is expanding and healing and is also good to do if you are feeling judgemental or inflexible about an issue.

Close your eyes, focus inwards and find yourself standing on the shores of a lake of shimmering rose-pink energy or water. Imagine a beautiful landscape around the lake, such as snowcapped mountains. Slowly step into the lake until the water rises up to your chest, then consciously bend your knees and float in the water, letting its energy suffuse you. The water supports you like the Red Sea. Imagine an opening in the crown of your head and let the pink water pour in here so that it courses through your body and out through the feet. You are lying in a river of pink energy. Revel in it. Then ground yourself, and come out of it.

Above **Nature never fails to provide inspiration for beginners attempting to master their visualization techniques.**

STIMULATING CREATIVITY

Creativity takes many different forms and it is latent in every person, although many people are not aware of their creative abilities. When you work creatively, the mind relaxes and focuses — which is very similar to the meditative process. Once you allow yourself to be creative, your heart and mind open to a spontaneous flow of positive energy; the mind automatically starts to work intuitively, accessing the deeper levels within the self.

Meditation benefits creativity by releasing thoughts and feelings which inhibit the flow of that creativity — and by stimulating inspiration. The more space you create by doing away with the mind's incessant activity, the more creativity is allowed to shine through.

Above **The most practical people will be surprised to find that they all have an element of creativity within them.**

CREATIVITY MEDITATION

Seat yourself comfortably and calm yourself with some deep breathing. You should have a strong sense of the time that's stretching out before you for this exercise — there is no pressure on you and no expectations from any source.

Imagine you are the most irrepressibly creative person and in front of you is a workshop where you can indulge your every whim. Every creative task imaginable is waiting to be tried — you can apply great, sweeping brushstrokes to a giant canvas, set about intricately cutting and layering sheets of decoupage paper, create a crazy design from tiny mosaic pieces, or bond together jewel-coloured shards of stained glass. You could even practise singing with a choir.

Be aware of your emotional response as you apply yourself to each creative task. Since it is only you who is present in this exercise in your mind, there should be no fear of being observed or judged.

Handling emotions

It is important to be aware of the power of your feelings. We often mask our true feelings — an appearance of calm which hides seething emotions; bravado when we are hurt or fearful; bottled up anger. In this way we are unconsciously affecting our own sense of wellbeing and others around us. If we are consumed by heated sentiments it is hard to be neutral and objective. We tend to become self-righteous, locked in our own opinion. This is the classic knee-jerk reaction — reactivity — the result of years of conditioning, the product of emotional patterns which, through repeated use have become so reinforced, they rise automatically.

However, meditation helps undo these patterns; it has the potential to turn around negativity, eventually healing your attitudes. When next your anger is aroused or someone hits an emotional nerve, try creating a gap, a small space in time before reacting. This allows you to briefly question the validity of your negative emotional reactions, to temporarily withhold judgements and criticisms. It lets you respond in a much more informed way rather than as a pure reflex action.

Once you can 'let go' of your reactivity, you are capable of reversing the entire thrust of your life. You are no longer giving credibility to your negative emotions. You realize that it is only you who infuses your thoughts, actions and reactions with their weight or level of importance. You invest them with meaning. It is therefore within your own power to reduce them to simple empty bubbles of energy. Without your subjective perceptions, they are inherently empty.

Emotions arising in meditation

Many of us are used to suppressing our real feelings, particularly anger. Unresolved conflicts and psychological issues become embedded in our subconscious, where they subliminally foster negative emotional states which ultimately prevent us from moving on in life. But as your meditation practice slowly clears away your mental chatter and creates space in your mind, you are giving the deeper issues that have been buried in your subconscious the chance to surface. It is as though a light shines into your inner being and your soul decides it is time for you to deal with those repressed feelings.

Such a transformation can't be defined by a single experience; it is a slow process in which a changing, perhaps heightened, awareness leads to the experiencing of new insights.

Left Anger, an emotion aptly reflected in the fiery glow of a sunset, is an issue most people grapple with today.

CLEARING EMOTIONS

One of the ways in which you can clear anger is to sit down and write a letter to the person you are angry with. Don't concern yourself with grammar and spelling and don't hold back on any of your feelings; simply pour out all your emotions on paper. Then put the letter away for two or three days (no longer). It is NOT intended for the recipient; it is only for your own personal clearing. Carefully read it, add anything you would like to, then put it away again for two or three days. Take it out once more, re-read it for the last time, then destroy it.

Otherwise, the following writing exercise is an excellent way to clear many emotional issues. These include control, perfectionism, self-sabotage, guilt, shame, self-pity, resentment, and judgment.

On a piece of paper write all your thoughts around the issue — the history, experiences, feelings. For instance, if you were clearing issues of anger, you would write what issue has caused that anger, why you're feeling angry, what thoughts and behaviour your emotional state is engendering. Then on another piece of paper rationalize whether you are justified in your anger.

Next, go to your meditation spot. Try to attain a meditative state and aim to connect with your higher self. You want to draw on your innate, intuitive wisdom, to tap into your higher self as it sees the whole picture in a detached, unemotional way — your role in the scenario, the role of others, how it serves you. Try to see that this is how the scenario was planned to happen, the reason why it did happen at this particular time, the feelings it created and where they came from. Finally burn all you have written on this issue, speaking words of release and letting go all the thoughts and feelings that need to be released.

If the head and body are to be healthy, you must begin by curing the mind.

— Plato

SELF-HEALING

Many people don't realize that they are able, through meditation and the body's own powerful self-healing mechanisms, to positively influence a state of mental and emotional wellbeing which filters through to a healthy, balanced physical body (see You are Energy on p56). The fact that the mind plays a great role in our health has been known for centuries by many cultures of the world, but this is only now becoming accepted in Western medicine. The mind can empower you to take a greater role in your own healing by stimulating the body's tremendous capacity for restoring itself to health.

Studies undertaken on the terminally ill show recoveries in those who channelled effort into positive thought and working on inner healing. This certainly does not mean you give up treating illness through an orthodox medical practitioner. It simply means that you enhance your medical healing by releasing negative conditions using positive affirmations and healing visualizations.

It is important to acknowledge that illness is often, in part, the result of past or immediate psychological factors that are causing an imbalance in the body's energy vibrations. Where energy is blocked in the body, this creates dysfunction. Emotions, thought patterns and spiritual beliefs are as important to one's health as the body's systems, tissues and organs. Good health is a realignment or balance between the physical body and mental, emotional and spiritual energy vibrations.

The path of meditation attempts to do away with apportioning 'blame', which is why it is important for you to fully accept — and like — who you are. If you can stop judging or being too hard on yourself, you are less likely to blame or judge others. Self-acceptance is important in your meditation practice as confidence, energy and happiness — and therefore good health — comes when you have the trust to accept your life and yourself without shame or embarrassment. By allowing yourself to look inward, you will learn to listen to the inner truths which come from your heart (the chakra centre of compassion — a quality meditation sets out to acquire).

Thoughts are a form of energy, where the emotions behind every thought will create vibrations that project an energy field, therefore a particular mindset can become a self-fulfilling prophecy. In this way, positive thought can help to keep you healthy. Indeed, studies have shown that the body's natural defence mechanisms are much stronger when you have a positive attitude.

Unbalanced emotions, attitudes and thoughts deplete natural physical energies and immunities so one is more likely to be susceptible to viruses and bacteria.

HEALING VISUALIZATION

Start in a comfortable position and do some initial deep breathing to centre yourself. Visualize that you are breathing in intense white light through the crown of your head, and it is flooding from your crown to your heart chakra. Feel the light filling and expanding your heart. As you exhale,

consciously release any tension, stress or pain. Try to intuitively feel any imbalance in energy, any irregularity in your tissues and cells, then direct the white light to that area. Imagine your cells and tissues being infused with the healing light. You can also imagine the cells changing in shape and size; then visualize them realigning and becoming balanced once again. As you exhale, imagine any toxins, diseased cells and tension being released from the body.

From the heart centre, direct the white light through the rest of your body, beginning with the left foot, moving on to the ankle, then the calf, and so on. Then direct it to the right leg. In a systematic way, fill up your entire body with light, imagining that you are a light being, energized, revitalized and healed. This process can be done at any time and can take anything from five minutes to an hour.

Below Buddhist teachings alert us to the idea of thoughts as energy, and that our thought processes affect our lives. Here, a flower laid at a Buddha's feet symbolizes a worshipper's desire to draw on the Buddha's powerful motivational spirit.

UNDERSTAND *what you are and what the world is, then only will fulfil-ment come.*

— Paul Brunton

A *retreat is not a refuge for escapists. It is an opportunity to deepen the inner life.*

— Natalia Baker

Go into the silence, For it is in the silence that all things unfold, In the silence you reach the heights, In the silence you are reborn, renewed, revitalized.

— Eileen Caddy

RETREATS

GOING ON A RETREAT

A retreat can be many things, depending on what you are looking for. The various forms of retreat range from spending quiet time in a beautiful location to the more formal, organized version where the primary aim is to remove yourself from distractions. This can be quite structured and will not suit everyone.

Generally retreats take the form of:

• Going away for a weekend on your own or with friends to meditate

• Two friends going away for the purpose of healing meditations, emotional processing and simply 'going with the flow'

• Solitude in Nature

• Formal, organized retreats in a meditation centre.

CHOOSING YOUR LOCATION

Monasteries, temples and churches often have retreat huts and cottages already set up with all the right facilities, and these can usually be hired for a reasonable fee. They are also often sited in beautiful locations. Although you are looking for simp-

Right The aromatic smell of incense, usually burned in honour of a deity, can heighten the senses in meditation.

licity, you do not want to exclude creativity and joyfulness — but it can be any spot that suffuses you with peace or lifts you emotionally, and which offers you relative seclusion and comfort.

Those who prefer simply to commune with Nature find that being immersed in the beauty of the outdoors reinforces their relationship with all living things and reminds them of their extraordinary connectedness with the universe. Also, being 'far from the madding crowd' in a place of peace and solitude allows you to practise mindfulness, and the colours, sounds and smells of Nature help to distract your attention from your incessant thoughts. Unhindered by the frenzy of your normal daily life, you are able to focus inward and take a hard, honest look at yourself. You will find, too, that as a result of your retreat and meditational practice, the people with whom you come into contact also benefit from your positive energies.

There is a story of a Yogi (a meditator having attained enlightenment through the practice of Yoga) on a retreat, who received a visit by another master dressed as a simple hermit. The master asked the Yogi what he was meditating on, and the Yogi replied, 'On patience'. The master was persistent and questioned the man further until at last the Yogi jumped up and shouted, 'Go away! Can't you see I'm busy?'

Below **Absolute solitude in Nature works by strengthening our feeling of oneness with the natural world around us.**

WHAT TO TAKE ON A RETREAT

Take cushions, mats and shawls to ensure that you will be as comfortable as possible. Make sure you include warm clothing because if you are cold, you will not be able to meditate properly. A clock is useful, too, to time your sessions.

Organized retreats have a pleasant ritual of starting and ending the meditation sessions by sounding a gong or bell. If you have arranged your own weekend, beautiful uplifting music can help to soothe you and create the right mood.

At formal retreats, leaders will expect participants to help out in terms of organizational duties throughout the event. This helps to create a friendly and co-operative rapport amongst the retreat members and benefits the smooth running of the event. Mindfulness during all such activities is encouraged so members deepen their awareness.

A TYPICAL DAY

If you have chosen to take part in an organized retreat, select one that offers an even mix of meditation and relaxation time. A timetable will usually be drawn up to provide some sense of structure to the retreat and will act as a guideline for activities. The sample here can be adapted to suit your needs.

Since beginners at meditation are not accustomed to spending many hours at inner contemplation, the length for a first-time retreat is generally a day or a weekend.

06:00	Rise and dress. Hot water.	½hr
07:30	Exercises, meditation or Tai Chi, Yoga, etc.	½hr
08:00	Breakfast: wholemeal porridge/fruit, tea/juice.	1hr
09:00	First main meditation session (seven minutes walking in-between).	1hr
10:00	Teatime: tea/juice, fruit/wholemeal cookies.	½hr
11:30	Free time until lunch or second main meditation session.	1hr
12:30	Lunch. Eat mindfully in silence.	1hr
13:30	Rest.	
14:00	Organized walk, swim, talk, etc. or third main meditation session.	2hrs
16:00	Teatime.	½hr
16:30	Main meditation session.	1hr
17:30	Free time until dinner.	1hr
18:30	Dinner.	1hr
19:30	Talk, related movie, etc. or main meditation session.	2hrs
21:30	Interviews or raising of issues with retreat master.	½hr
22:00	Lights out. No talking.	

Above After practising regularly, you will find that you have a natural time span for your meditation, and you will tend to come out of it naturally.

TIME OUT FOR YOURSELF

EATING MEDITATION

Because perfect health is dependent on body, mind and spirit being in balance and harmony, your daily diet plays an important role. On a retreat, sustenance should be simple, tasty and light. You don't want to feel sluggish from large, heavy meals; these can leave you feeling uncomfortable, particularly before a meditation session because your body's energies are harnessed to the digestive processes. Select easily digestible foods such as fresh fruits, salads, soups, steamed or lightly sautéed vegetables, nutritious pulses and grains, and white meat such as chicken, or fish.

Ideal refreshments are fresh, slightly diluted juices, green or herbal teas and spring water.

You can also make the act of eating a form of meditation. Turn every meal into a special ritual by including fresh flowers. As you eat, mindfully observe the colour and appearance of the particular food on your plate. Heighten your senses — be aware of aroma, appreciate how the food tastes, the flavours and texture. Be aware of the consistency while you eat and notice how long the flavours remain in your mouth.

This is good, once again, for focusing the mind and ensuring that you are fully present in the moment.

Above **The freshness, appearance and visual presentation of your meals will make a vast difference to your enjoyment of it. Adding flowers to the table also creates an atmosphere.**

THE BENEFITS OF SILENCE

If you are serious about your meditation retreat, you will want as little distraction as possible from your normal demanding routine. So you may choose to leave behind your cellphone, laptop computer and portable TV. Being attuned to silence and the sounds of Nature can be very powerful and uplifting to the soul. Re-establishing your oneness with all living things is revitalizing, leaving you restful but energized. If you are used to being surrounded by a constant flux of noise, people and action, the silence can be unsettling. This is where an experienced retreat master will be able to guide you and help you adjust your perspective.

This may also be the time when your soul decides to release some of your deeply buried emotional issues. Don't be embarrassed; allow the feelings to come up, acknowledge them and then release them. The retreat master will offer guidance and will listen, feel empathy and give advice. He or she is trained to handle such emotional issues when they arise. You will find, too, that the people together with you on the retreat can also offer loving and caring support.

Left **Being 'in tune' with the outdoors uplifts and refreshes mind and body.**

A PERSONAL EXPERIENCE OF AN INFORMAL RETREAT

"For a few years now my dear friend Jenny and I have arranged an informal eight-day retreat in a simple rustic cottage on the bank of a lagoon, near the sea and surrounded by hills. The first of these retreats was motivated by the death of my husband of 30 years during an intensive period of teaching meditation. I continued presenting courses, but was close to collapse, having delayed the natural process of grieving. The effect of that first retreat was so profoundly healing, strengthening and uplifting that we decided it

Above **Focusing on a candle flame is a useful tool that helps you create an inner stillness within yourself.**

would become part of our annual schedule. Our intention during this time is to deepen our meditation practice, and clear emotional blockages and other issues through writing and visualization processes. Each retreat takes on its own character with different emphases, although long walks are a consistent feature, as is the joy of laughter and fun, delectable meals, the deep sharing of our lives and purpose, and the occasional brief visit to the nearby town for groceries and a meal.

The experience of 'going with the flow' is magical. Normally, our lives are structured and directed by demands of work, family and the complexities of modern living. In my own life, because of the nature of my work with people, 20 telephone calls means it has been an easy day. My e-mail system has been known to collect 200 messages in five days!

The retreat offers freedom from all this. We rest at ease in a deeper part of ourselves, touching into intuitive guidance and feelings. These allow us to be finely attuned to what is appropriate at any time. We observe how, as we follow this inner guidance, our daily activities are always in perfect balance: exercise, length of meditations, when to talk or be silent, to be serious or to laugh, to be together or alone. There is a sense of 'rightness' to it all. I remember saying one day that it felt as though we were under grace. 'Going with the flow' has deepened our sense of trust in our own inner wisdom, which knows more than the rational mind could ever conceive.

Our meditations are deep and powerful. We derive new understandings, perceptions and experiences of who we really are as we touch into expanded levels of consciousness. The peace becomes 'the peace that passeth all understanding' and our hearts open with love and compassion.

The effect of these meditations and the experience of these eight days is accumulative, and two revitalized women return home, appreciably more conscious, joyful and serene."

— Natalia Baker

HOW MEDITATION ENHANCES YOUR LIFE

Our world is becoming increasingly claustrophobic with the steadily growing populations of the big cities, restricted living space, the constant ebb and flow of traffic, and the effects of industrial pollution and the thinning ozone layer. This, and the inexorable pace of life because of improved technology, can distract you from listening to your heart — to your inner voice — particularly when you are bombarded with views and opinions from advertising, the media, colleagues, friends and relatives. It is up to you to create the space for this innate truth and inner wisdom to emerge. Meditation teaches you to face your inner space rather than blocking it by surrounding yourself with comfort food and drink, conversation, music, television, and material possessions.

Many people are experiencing a general dissatisfaction and are struggling to find permanent happiness or

Above **The skills you gain in learning to meditate will prove invaluable to your abilities of achieving a state of absolute relaxation.**

fulfilment in their lifestyle. We place great value on materialism today, but many people are discovering that owning a luxury mansion or an expensive sportscar does not quite satisfy all of their inner needs. The mindfulness,

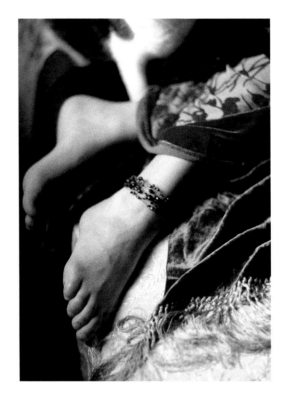

tranquillity and insight that meditation brings about teaches us to achieve a sense of freedom and well-being arising from spiritual happiness. This is possible when you have learnt to know and understand yourself, and accept who you are with your strengths and failings.

To define 'What is meditation?' cannot be done in one sentence. Meditation is many things: a concentration technique that helps focus the mind

on one thing at a time; the abandoning of rationality and logical processes to allow intuition to expand the horizons of the mind; rejecting the habitual patterns of your conditioned lifestyle and opening up to invite in fresh perspectives; realizing that you can change your life simply by empowering yourself because it is your mind that determines how you see the world.

Put simply, meditation is remaining with a highly tuned awareness in the present.

Meditation can also lead to very personal experiences which are difficult to verbalize or even to fully understand. This is possibly why it is not easy to define. Some people describe their meditational experiences as spiritual (not necessarily in a religious context), others as moments of intense realizations, windows to a greater consciousness.

What meditation does do is add an extra dimension to your life by contributing to a personal inner transformation that makes you see your world from a fresh perspective. As Gary Snyder is so aptly quoted by Joseph Goldstein in the book *Voices of Insight*: 'There is a world behind the world we see that is the same world but more open, more transparent.'

'BEING IN THE MOMENT'

Remember that your inner life will dictate your outer life, so moments of tension or pent-up frustration need to be worked through effectively to dispel the negative energies.

When there is an emotional or tension build-up, you can make a suitable retreat spot wherever you are: the 'chapel' in airports is a great place in which to meditate; in your office at work (with the door closed); in the car in a traffic jam; in waiting rooms; in queues; on a bus.

Apply the awareness technique wherever you are. Take three slow, deep breaths and try to turn your mind into a positive state. Heighten your senses by being aware of — but not lingering on — any smells around you (particularly if you're outdoors); be aware of sounds by letting them come to you but don't latch on to them; look around you at everyone and everything. Notice everything as if for the very first time, but don't focus on anything in particular. Don't force the process, stay relaxed.

Saying a personal mantra or an affirmation to yourself can help to keep you aware and in the presence of the moment, for example: 'I am relaxed, calm and peaceful. I stay in the now with effortless ease.'

Below **The frenzied pace of modern life makes it increasingly necessary for us to 'take time out', and being faced with the 'larger than life' elements of Nature helps put our daily stresses into perspective.**

YOUR mental state should always remain calm. Even if some anxiety occurs, as it is bound to in life, you should always be calm. Like a wave, which rises from the water and dissolves back into the water, these disturbances are very short, so they should not affect your basic mental attitude. If you remain calm your blood pressure and so on remains more normal and as a result your health will improve.

— Dalai Lama's Book of Wisdom

THIS is your life and nobody is going to teach you, no book, no guru. Learn from yourself, not from books. It is an endless thing, a fascinating thing and when you learn about your self from yourself, out of that learning wisdom comes. Then you can live a most extraordinary, happy, beautiful life.

— Krishnamurti

MEDITATION IN MOVEMENT

Skilful activity

THE nature of these controlled activities allows them to be likened to the meditative state — they encourage the mind to focus and turn inward instead of emphasizing physical action. This demands greater precision and a more focused involvement in the physical activity, leading to relaxation and meditational benefits. Some of the following training methods are angled toward fitness and health, some to aligning the body's subtle energies, others simply to creativity. There is a multitude of videos, books and classes which will enable you to expand your knowledge and explore these activities further.

They are especially good for Western-oriented tendencies toward speed, action and adrenaline. These practices coerce us into doing some meditation while we are busy learning a graceful movement, focusing on muscle control or creating a beautiful flower arrangement. The practices are all part of much larger systems of philosophy, but we can still derive much benefit from doing them, nonetheless.

Although the examples here have been in existence in some cases for thousands of years (Yoga and Chi Kung) and in others to just a few decades (Aikido), they all require a focused mind. During the early practice phases of these contemplative activities, you need to develop a mindfulness that matches the mindfulness of meditation. Later, when you become more accomplished, you are able to introduce a more expanded awareness to your state of mind. As with meditation, mindfulness leads to awareness, so these practices are good as preliminary or supplementary activities to your efforts at meditating.

Beyond the beauty, peace and integrative aspects of the activity is the potential for you to open up to your inner wisdom. The Buddhist teaching is that real wisdom is born of two main characteristics: compassion and skilful activity. It is a wisdom gained through a love of the process of learning — not the end product. And it is our kindness toward, and acceptance of, ourselves that leads us to living a life that is honest and truthful.

The joy and love that arises then spills over into the lives of others — because you project outwardly what is going on inwardly, a sense of balance, happiness and love for who you are and where you are in your life is going to vibrate positively to those around you. It is the simple and real meaning of true wisdom.

Left Any activity that requires focus and concentration, such as this Chinese girl working at calligraphy, will bring the individual towards a meditative state.

Yoga

This is an ancient Vedic form of contemplative exercise, developed in India around 3000BCE (the Vedas are the sacred, ancient Sanskrit writings of Hinduism). It is a system that promotes health and wellbeing by helping to align and build positive subtle energies in a person, and it generates a meditative state of mind through focused concentration and controlled breathing. The philosophy of Yoga is similar to the Chinese notion of Yin and Yang, where negative and positive energies are interdependent on one another and strive to create balance.

Yoga hinges on body postures called *asanas*, which are used to massage, stimulate and tone all parts of the body. Revitalization and strengthening occur not only in the muscles and bones but also in organs and systems (nervous, endocrine, respiratory, muscular). Tension and stiffness is worked through and energy trapped in the body is released.

With the help of an instructor you can isolate areas of the body where movement has been either restricted or overemphasized, for which you can practise certain postures to remedy the imbalance. The calm and relaxing nature of the poses plus the need to focus single-pointedly while doing each one also helps introduce a meditative state of mind.

Yoga's gentle nature is especially good for those who find straight meditation too rigorous. The intention is not to hurry, force or strain the postures and they bring much benefit if done regularly and mindfully.

A YOGA EXERCISE: THE COBRA

The Cobra as a posture has very good general benefits. It works the vertebrae which is the major carrier for the body's nervous and subtle energy systems and is excellent for the back muscles and abdominal organs.

First remove any spectacles, watch, and jewellery. Lie face down on a mat or carpet (forehead touching the mat) with the arms and elbows lying alongside the body, hands palms down with fingers to either side of the chin, in line with the shoulders (1).

Slowly raise the head, shoulders and then the trunk by pushing down on the hands (2). As the arms straighten, your vertebrae will form a tighter curve. In the final posture, the arms are fully extended, the head back and the lower abdomen is touching the floor (3) — but only raise yourself as high as is comfortable for you. The movement must be done very slowly so that you bend one vertebra at a time. Hold the final posture for a count of 15 seconds while allowing the mind to focus on and really feel the sensation of being in the posture. Then slowly reverse the movement and rest for a minute or so. Repeat one more time.

CHI KUNG

Chi Kung (also known as qigong), literally meaning 'energy exercises', was developed in northern China over 6000 years ago. It is based on the notion of *chi*, or the vital energy-force, which is key to the Indian, Tibetan and Chinese medical systems. Like electricity, flowing *chi* energy is invisible but carries incredible power. The skilful guiding of this nurturing energy through your being enables you to attain balance, harmony and any healing that is necessary. This is achieved through normally short physical exercises, with emphasis on the breath and concentration.

The concept of Yin and Yang, or balance of opposites, is applied to the three main elements of Chi Kung. These elements consist of:
— a calm but alert state of mind to help focus concentration
— deep but natural breathing to increase and circulate *chi* energy
— posture (a straight back) and/or movement.

You need to see this process as a progression; first you should try to relax and calm the mind a little before doing these exercises as you need a restful mind to breathe correctly. Secondly, the deep, calm breathing (done in a positive state of mind) gathers chi. Correct posture and the movements, which may include visualizations together with the breathing, then help guide the *chi* along the correct channels. It may sound complicated initially, but once you have become familiar with the exercises, they will feel very natural, easy and can even be exhilarating.

A CHI KUNG EXERCISE: CARRYING THE MOON

This particular exercise is good for the spine, invigorating it and the main energy channel, or meridian, that runs parallel to it; *chi* is radiated outward from here, along the length of the entire body. This exercise engenders youthfulness and sexual vitality.

Start in a comfortable standing position. Drop your hands to just below the knees by bending your body forward in a smooth curve, with your head following the arc. Remain relaxed for a few seconds, visualizing *chi* energy rising up the central channel, along the vertebrae, to the crown of your head.

Slowly straighten the body, at the same time raising and straightening the arms forward then upward while breathing in. When your outstretched arms and hands are at their zenith, with you looking at them, form a full-moon shape with thumbs and index fingers. For balance the body should be slightly curved forward and the head gently thrown back. Hold your breath for a few seconds while in this position. Finally, as you breathe out, lower the arms to your sides and straighten your body.

During this out-breath, visualize *chi* as liquid light cascading from your crown, through your body and into the ground; see this as pure energy that washes out all your bad thoughts and negative emotions.

Right **Qi (chi) means 'subtle life-force', gong implies 'repeated labour' — thus it could be loosely translated as 'repetition of energy work'. Essentially, you are connecting with universal energy.**

TAI CHI CHUAN

A Taoist monk developed Tai Chi Chuan (or Yin-Yang boxing) around 800 years ago as a branch of Chi Kung. It was primarily used as a sophisticated form of self-defence in which force was not used on the opponent or attacker, rather his or her energy was reflected back at him/her. With this form of movement, the highly trained mind and body of the defender uses his mastery over *chi* (life-force) to effortlessly outwit the opponent. Calm, speed and oneness with *chi* are combined to create a space into which the attacker 'falls' and becomes tired and confused. Today, the grace and beauty of the movements have strongly caught the atten-

tion of Western tradition. This practice, especially, needs to be learned from a master since it is a string of a number of Chi Kung exercises that flow into each other in a normally slow and gentle movement.

Learning to adopt a correct standing posture is an important part of Tai Chi; body weight needs to be evenly distrib-

Above **In Tai Chi, the focus is internal, turning inward on the mind and concentrating on being fully relaxed rather than employing the use of force and strength.**

uted across both legs. This posture is then maintained when arm movements are introduced, and later when breathing is coordinated with the sequence of moves. An improved posture helps alleviate back problems and reduces the chance of future problems developing.

Also, practising correct abdominal breathing results in an increased oxygen supply to the lungs and therefore the body, and at the same time helps relax the body and ease muscular tensions. Concentration is required to correctly perform Tai Chi; it therefore helps to focus and divert the mind from daily mental stresses and anxieties.

A TAI CHI EXERCISE: RAISING AND LOWERING OF HANDS

For the correct stance, stand with feet hip-width apart, knees slightly bent, back straight, and rest the hands lightly on the thighs. To make sure you perform the sequence correctly, try it out first against a wall or flat surface. Stand at arm's length from the wall so that you can place both hands flat on the surface, then lower your hands to your sides. Move the arms straight out towards the wall till the backs of the fingers lightly brush it. The wrists should lead with the fingers trailing as you slide your hands up the surface. When the wrists reach shoulder height, change direction to move down the surface, once again leading with the wrists, the fingers angled away from you. When you feel they are about to break surface contact with the wall, stop moving the hands downward. This is the position (it should be in line with the hips) at which you should start to lift the arms, and to which you lower them again. When lowering the hands, sink slightly lower in the legs. Shoulders and elbows should remain relaxed throughout the exercise.

Now try out the sequence away from the flat surface, coordinating abdominal breathing with the movements. Breathe in as you start to move the hands out, continuing till the wrists are at shoulder level; then breathe out as the hands move down to hip level. Return hands to their original position on your thighs and repeat the sequence.

AIKIDO

Aikido – 'the art of peace' – was developed by the great Japanese master Morihei Ueshiba (1883–1969). It technically falls within the martial arts field, but its methods make it also a very successful means to self-discovery. Aikido's ethics and philosophy are pivotal to the effectiveness of this martial art.

Aikido practitioners don't spar, take part in tournaments or competitions, and they insist that they do not 'fight'.

Aikido teaches many movements and techniques but the real mastery comes from years of nurturing values such as nonaggression, maintaining a calm state of mind in an extreme situation, not being concerned with either winning or losing, and so on. All this enhances the practitioner's awareness and sensitivity towards his or her opponent, enabling the practitioner to reroute the opponent's attacking energy with the least possible force. Rather than being reactive, the practitioner is proactive. Where there is aggression, he is continually willing to de-escalate the conflict rather than overpower his opponent with some type of force.

Because Aikido practitioners remain calm and unafraid, and clearly in touch with their intuition, they therefore remain open to whatever move is made.

Through extensive breathing exercises and much training, the practitioner's mind becomes single-focused, engendering a good meditative state of mind. It is this state of mind that allows for the development of the necessary qualities in the 'peaceful warrior'.

So once more, the universal laws of creating peace, space and lightness are the key to balancing our lives.

Above right **What Eastern exercises have in common is a supreme degree of control over body, mind and spirit – stimulating the free flow of** *chi*, **our life-force.**

AN EXERCISE IN AIKIDO

An emotional argument is a good example of of how taking an inflexible and/or aggressive stand escalates conflict. It is easy to want the power or authority to force people's views, but this need is the result of ego. Aikido challenges the practitioner to find his 'true' intent in a situation. Ideally, one needs to reach a point where the following exercise comes instinctively the next time you find yourself in an argument.

Try to stay calm and breathe deeply. Resist a knee-jerk reaction, and take the time to study your own true intentions. Try not to focus on the specifics. Analyze your intentions – are you feeling fear, aggression, or are you upholding your reputation or pride? This can give you great insight into your own mind and into the whole process of conflict, and reveal alternative ways in which to handle it other than your initial non-thinking gut response. Aikido uses similar principles but on a faster, physical level.

DANCE

Dance is one of the very few naturally spontaneous things we still do today and which are good for the soul — our general wellbeing benefits from the spontaneity, freedom, and joy that dance provides. In India, dance takes on the role of a prayer for the dancer.

To gain real and lasting benefit, contemplative dance or movement demands great awareness. There needs to be a meaningful, sensitive response to the music and the body in order to move consciousness into peace and harmony.

AN EXERCISE IN DANCE

Choose a piece of music that is energizing and uplifting to you — it can be anything from modern techno-beat to jazz or soul. The key factors for your dance movements are spontaneity and freedom of body (but with intense awareness).

Move your arms around your torso and above your head, twist and bend your torso to stimulate the energy flow and bring it into harmony with all the different parts of your body. You can feel the increased energy being channelled through your arms and legs, up your spine, and into your chest and lungs. You are expressing who and what you are in a universal language that needs no words. Dance is your communication.

By moving intuitively and fluidly without controlling the movement, you release and free yourself, getting in touch with who you are.

Below **Dance can be used as a means of expressing deep emotions without words. It can release pent-up energy or can simply be a joyful moment.**

I live within the light
I love within the light
I laugh within the light
I am sustained and nourished
by the light
I joyously serve the light for
I AM the light
I AM...

THE TEA CEREMONY

People who learn of the Japanese Tea Ceremony for the first time may think it sounds like an unnecessary complex ritual, but the idea behind it is actually quite simple.

The Taoist or Chinese tea ceremony is a little more relaxed and mostly has to do with beauty and harmony, but the Zen monks go one step further: for them, conceptualized notions of beauty are not presented obviously. There is more emphasis on simplicity, and the precision of movement, or ritual, which encourages a certain clarity in the mind in an effort to bring it closer to its purest nature.

Today, the West is now well versed in the health and medicinal benefits of Chinese green tea. Quality is the key. There is beauty in hue and taste, and, like a Zen painting, it also seems to lift and lighten the spirit. Compare this with how many of us mask our coffee with cream and sugar. Green tea, in its simplicity invites you into 'empty' space – and to become a part of it. This is the essence of the tea ceremony itself. It is the mindfulness of your actions, and being aware of each moment of the tea-making and tea-drinking ritual that turns it into a meditative process.

A CHINESE TEA CEREMONY

Find a comfortable, uncluttered space in- or outdoors. Add an object of beauty like a simple flower arrangement, statue or picture. The sound of running or bubbling water is good. Make a cup of tea very slowly and carefully, with attention to detail, but stay completely relaxed. If you can, use simple but beautiful ceramics, no plastic kettle (since it gives off chemicals in hot water) and a good quality tea. Once the tea has steeped and you are ready to drink it, fully savour the beauty in the colour, the aroma and taste of the tea, and your surroundings. Breathe in the lightness and beauty you have created for yourself. The ethic behind this is that when you make the world around you peaceful, beautiful and enlightened, your heart and mind follow suit.

Below Experiencing the Eastern concept of a tea ceremony offers us an excellent exercise in mindfulness. If we apply ourselves to the ritual with focused concentration, it can be likened to a meditation, particularly since it engages most of our senses – appearance, smell, taste, sensation and, if in a garden, sounds around us.

Ikebana

Ikebana, meaning 'the art of placement' or 'the living art', is the Japanese decorative art of flower arrangement. It originated in China around 810CE in the form of elaborate and beautiful offerings placed in temples. Later it spread as a contemplative art among noble families, and since then has spread rapidly around the world. Today there are over 2000 schools of ikebana, the four main ones being the Japanese schools Sogetsu, Ichiyo, Ikenobu and Ohara.

The incredible diversity of styles today makes it difficult to isolate even a common denominator linking them all, but the principles behind them remain the same.

In learning the art of ikebana, you are working with a microcosm of your world. Many of the schools of thought today still embrace the age-old principle of balance which exists in the trilogy of heaven, man and earth. Within this concept, heaven represents all our lofty and good intentions, which are embodied in our icons of God or gods, gurus and other revered figures of our personal universe. The earth keeps us grounded in the reality of our everyday life on earth. Humans create the balance between these two opposites, where, in their efforts to strive toward the incredible potential

all human beings have, they first need to experience being fully human.

This trilogy acts as a guide to the placement of flowers and leaves in a container — in sets of three — to mirror the balance of dynamism and harmony that exists in heaven, man and earth. The largest background pieces represent heaven, the middle components man, with the lowest, foreground elements representing earth. One needs to create harmony between the vessel that holds the water, the water that nourishes the plants, and the plants that add beauty to our lives. Beauty should not only please the eye, but also should help you to connect with the beauty that exists in all of us by stirring a positive emotional response. The metaphor is very important, especially when it is positive. You also start to realize that you can be in touch with nature so much more easily than you think — you don't have to go on an expensive trip to a nature reserve but can simply become 'one' with Nature through the beautiful, simple act of arranging some flowers.

Left **Although ikebana is recognized as a Japanese art, it has its roots in China. It is based on the triangle of man and his relationship to heaven**

An ikebana exercise: freestyle

Freestyle is actually more difficult than a 'form' exercise, but the difficulty is only in learning to trust your inner creativity — which is inherent in all of us. Select a good container that will match the flowers, twigs, plants, or whatever you have chosen to use. Look at the container and first try placing the flowers in your mind's eye. You can also hold them up near the vase before you cut them to make sure the stems will be the right lengths. Take time to notice the quiet, detailed beauty of each plant and try to get a 'feel' for how it would sit next to another. Stay relaxed and don't get impatient. Take a whole morning or afternoon to do one arrangement. Tea and quiet music can also create a wonderful mood.

Since you don't have the constraints of a more formal approach, lose yourself in the process if you can. Try not to make the arrangement for anyone else's approval. Simply make it for yourself.

and earth (echoed in many cultures of the world). The idea is that each arrangement features three tiers, corresponding to man, heaven and earth.

Contacts

WORLD WIDE ONLINE MEDITATION CENTER
11400 4th St. N. #310
St. Petersburg, FL 33716
Tel: +1 (727) 576-1800
E-Mail:
jmalloy@meditationcenter.com
Website: www.meditationcenter.com

MEDITATION SOCIETY OF AMERICA
PO Box 13, Gradyville, PA 19039
USA
Tel: +1 (610) 696-8432
E-mail:
medit8@meditationsociety.com
Website: www.meditationsociety.com

THE AMERICAN MEDITATION INSTITUTE
PO Box 430, Averill Park, NY 12018
USA
Tel: +1 (518) 674-8714
E-mail: postmaster@american-
meditation.org
Website:
www.americanmeditation.org/

**JON KABAT-ZINN CENTER
FOR MINDFULNESS**
55 Lake Avenue North
Worcester, MA 01655
Tel: +1 (508) 856-2656
E-mail: mindfulness@umassmed.edu
Website:
www.umassmed.edu/cfm/life/zinn.cfm

THE GAWLER FOUNDATION
PO Box 77G
Yarra Junction, Victoria 3797
South Australia
Tel: +61 (03) 5967-1730
Fax: +61 (03) 5967-1715
E-mail: info@gawler.asn.au
Website: www.gawler.asn.au/

NON-SECTARIAN MEDITATION CENTRE
280 Hay Street, Subiaco WA 6064
Western Australia
Tel: +61 (08) 9381-4877
Website:
www.buddhanet.net/ozmed.htm

SELF-REALIZATION FELLOWSHIP
(Tradition: Yoga Meditation)
3880 San Rafael Avenue, Dept. 9W
Los Angeles, CA 90065-3298, USA
Tel: +1 (323) 342-0247
Fax: +1 (323) 225-5088
Website: www.yogananda-srf.org

**SIVANANDA YOGA VEDANTA INTERNATIONAL
CENTRES**
(Tradition: Yoga Meditation)
Website: www.sivananda.org

**BRAHMA KUMARIS WORLD SPIRITUAL
ORGANIZATIONS**
(Tradition: Raja Yoga Meditation)
All countries at: www.db.bkwsu.com

ACEM MEDITATION
PB 2559 Solli, N-0202 Oslo, Norway
Tel: +47 23-11-87-00
Fax: +47 22-83-18-31
E-mail: acem@acem.com
Website: www.acem.com

**SHAMBHALA NETWORK OF MEDITATION
CENTERS**
1084 Tower Road
Halifax, Nova Scotia B3H 2Y5,
Canada
Tel: +1 (902) 420-1118
E-mail: info@shambhala.org
Website: www.shambhala.org

INSIGHT MEDITATION SOCIETY HOMEPAGE
(Tradition: Buddhist – Vipassana/
Theravada)
1230 Pleasant Street, Barre MA 01005
Massachusetts, USA
Tel: +1 (978) 355-4378
Fax: +1 (978) 355-6398
Website: www.dharma.org/ims.htm
or
www.insightmeditation.org/friends_of
_gaia_house_internatio.htm
Website:
www.dhamma.org/wclist.htm

TRADITION OF SAYAGYI U BA KHIN
(Vipassana/Theravada Buddhism)
Website: www.ubakhin.com

NOTE: Wherever possible, meditation centres featured here offer non-sectarian teachings and websites list worldwide contact addresses.

INDEX

ACKNOWLEDGMENTS

New Holland Publishers would like to thank Sharon and Charles Gosling for offering their elegant home, Montacute, to us for our photo shoot, and Brian and Theresa Aldridge, who lent us their beachfront home; photographer Nick Aldridge for the magic he created through his lens; our model Nicci Ressel for her calmness and serenity; and Simon Rhodes for his good-natured assistance in styling the shoots.

Also, thanks to Halogen for the generous use of their gorgeous fabrics and Claudine of Namasté Yoga and Exercise Wear for lending us their beautiful garments.

Mariëlle Renssen would like to thank Natalia Baker for her permission to use material from her Meditation Course manual, and for her valuable contributions to the text.

It has been a real privilege — and an enormous amount of fun! — to work with Natalia. She is so very wise, warm and wonderful, and quite simply the most inspiring person I've ever worked with.

Finally, thanks to designer Sheryl Buckley who, visually, has done great justice to the spirit of meditation by creating this absolutely beautiful book.

We gratefully acknowledge *Bag of Jewels*, Hayward Books (Australia) and *The Dalai's Lama's Book of Wisdom*, Thorsons (London) for snippets of wisdom on pp36, 54, and 78; and p78 respectively.

PHOTOGRAPHIC CREDITS

All photography by Nicholas Aldridge for NHIL, with the exception of the following photographers and/or agencies (copyright rests with these individuals and/or their agencies). NHIL = New Holland Image Library

4–5	Great Stock	27	Craig Fraser	71	Caroline Jones
7c	NHIL/Massimo Cecconi	29	Craig Fraser	72	Dinodia Picture Library
7d	NHIL/Massimo Cecconi	30	NHIL/Ryno Reyneke	73	NHIL/Massimo Cecconi
7f	NHIL/Massimo Cecconi	31	NHIL/Massimo Cecconi	74	Dugald Bremner Studio
7g	NHIL/Massimo Cecconi	36	Nicholas Aldridge	76	NHIL/Massimo Cecconi
8–9	Frantisek Stuad	40	David Wall	77	NHIL/Massimo Cecconi
12	Great Stock	46	Hutchison Library	80	Frantisek Stuad
13	Werner Forman Archive	48b	Great Stock	81	NHIL/Ryno Reyneke
14a	Sylvia Cordaiy Photo Library	49	Nigel Hicks	82	Nicholas Aldridge
b	Nigel Hicks	50	Frantisek Stuad	84	NHIL/Ryno Reyneke
18	Gallo/Getty Images	58	Sylvia Cordaiy Photo Library	85	NHIL/Ryno Reyneke
19	David Wall	61	Andy Belcher	86	Scott Aitken
21	Great Stock	62	Great Stock	87	Photo Access
22	Francoise Sauze/Science Photo Library	63	Andy Belcher	88 a	Gallo/Getty Images
		64	Gallo/Getty Images	89	Frantisek Stuad
23	David Wall	65	Robin Smith	90	Frantisek Stuad
24	Nicholas Aldridge	67	Andy Belcher	92–93	Andy Belcher
26	Robin Smith	70	Sean O'Toole		